Sascha Lasserson: Portrait of a Teacher

Sascha Lasserson
Portrait of a Teacher

Reminiscences of Sascha by his pupils

Edited by
Michael Lasserson

Kahn and Averill
London

First published in 2005 by
Kahn & Averill
9 Harrington Road, London SW7 3ES

British Library Cataloguing in Publication Data
A catalogue record for this book is available from the British Library

ISBN 1 871 082 83 8

Set in 10.5pt Quadraat
Book design by Simon Stern

Contents

Introduction

Sascha Lasserson died more than twenty years ago and during this period the idea of some sort of memoir or biography of him has been suggested more than once. The Lasserson Trust has done wonderful work in perpetuating his memory, as have his pupils in their teaching and playing, but such endeavours cannot adequately convey the essence of the man – his brilliance as both teacher and performer, his kindness and his warmth of personality.

This book, a collection of reminiscences of Sascha by his pupils, attempts to do just that as they pay loving homage to his memory. Their contact with Sascha linked them with the Auer tradition and with that incredible class of which he was so illustrious a member. Surely no-one can forget the photograph of that class, in pride of place on the piano, with Auer massive and bearded among his pupils – and with Sascha sitting on the floor in the front row...

The genesis of the book, that which gave the whole thing a kickstart, was an observation by my wife. As an Associated Board Examiner for many years she had become used to meeting musicians all over the country who, on hearing her name, would at once ask if she was related to Sascha. But gradually she became aware that such queries were becoming less frequent as a generation of players and teachers grew up who knew nothing of Sascha, of what he represented and of what he achieved. It prompted a feeling of urgency that a book such as this should be published, an anthology of vivid memories, not only of a great teacher but also of a great artist and a remarkable human being who became guide, philosopher, and friend to all his pupils. For those who knew him this composite portrait of Sascha will serve to reunite them with each other as well as with him; for those who never knew him it will serve as an introduction to an almost mythic age of musicians and of music-making.

It has been a privilege to work on this collection and I have to thank all those who gave up time to prepare and submit their contributions, generously allowing me to edit as I thought fit. It is indeed sad to note the passing of six of the contributors – Lionel Bentley, Angela Dale, Daphne Ibbott, Harry Legge, Robert Lewin and Jack Rothstein, – since the inception of the project.

Where possible I have included a brief curriculum vitae for each contributor for, collectively, they constitute a history of violin-teaching in this country, and I thank those who added to their contributions in this way.

I am most grateful to Brian Underwood, who has devoted so much time and effort to the Lasserson Trust, for help with certain editorial problems (including the music excerpts) and for access to valuable archive material. His encouragement has been echoed by Tessa Robbins–Khambatta while she was, herself, shouldering the burden of running the Trust. I thank Emanuel Hurwitz, who – together with his wife Kay – generously hosted a meeting of several of Sascha's old pupils, whose reminiscences were beautifully recorded for us by David Van Dyl. Thanks are due to Tully Potter for his historical overview of the St Petersburg Conservatoire, and I thank Ann Measures for many helpful suggestions regarding layout and for securing a most important contribution for me. Both present and past editors of *The Strad* have been generous in their help, with Naomi Sadler allowing me to trawl through the photographic archives, and Joanna Pieters allowing me to use material previously published in the journal, notably Max Jaffa's account of his meeting with Sascha (which led to Max's eventual rehabilitation as a violinist) as well as a profile of Sascha by Robert Lewin.

The staff of the Newspaper Library at Colindale; the Library of the Royal College of Music; the Barbican Music Centre; and the

Archive department of the Wigmore Hall all assisted with various searches. The BBC Written Archives Centre at Caversham have kindly permitted us to reproduce details of Sascha's broadcast programmes as well as his photograph, and Mr Neil Summerville of that Unit gave invaluable help in tracing the information in the Radio Times Archives. I also tried to trace reviews of Sascha's performance of the Spohr Concerto No 9 which he played in Helsingfors when he was ten with Kajanus conducting – but, alas, without success despite the best efforts of the Finnish Music Centre and the Music Library of Helsinki University.

I must thank my son David for his contribution about Sascha's pupil, Johnny Van Derrick, and for his help with the music excerpts. Georgie Robins prepared the manuscript for submission to the publishers, and I am grateful for all her hard work. I thank, too, Miss Kate Clanchy of the department of Modern Languages at Dulwich College for preparing the translation of Sascha's Diploma, and Miss Jamila Gavin for her efforts to trace film of Sascha.

Our publisher, Mr Morris Kahn and the book's designer, Mr Simon Stern, have been towers of strength with much tactful prompting throughout the book's overlong gestation. Lastly, I acknowledge with gratitude my wife Nadia's role as catalyst in getting the whole project started.

MICHAEL LASSERSON

Auer, the Conservatoire and Sascha - an overview
by Tully Potter

The early years of Sascha Lasserson's life, the years which laid the foundations of a life of solid achievement, seem at first glance to have been little different from those of many other members of what we call the 'Leopold Auer School'. It soon becomes apparent, however, that he was a somewhat unusual pupil. In an age when musical virtuosi were routinely cut adrift by their teachers and sent out into the profession in their early teens, he had his first major success at the Imperial Conservatory in St Petersburg – the award of a Gold Medal – in 1909, when he was 19; and when he graduated with a certificate of Highest Distinction in 1911, he was 21. At that stage he had been a serious student for eleven years and had already been playing in public for more than a decade. Before considering what kind of education he received, let us relate his experience to that of some of his contemporaries.

Born on May Day 1890, Lasserson was one year older than Adolf Busch, two years older than Joseph Szigeti and three years older than Franz von Vecsey. Busch began playing the violin at three but did not have decent tuition until he was 11 and just about to enter the Cologne Conservatory – from which he graduated as a soloist, chamber musician and composer when he was not yet 18. Szigeti had excellent early lessons from an uncle and went to Hubay at the Budapest Academy when he was 11, playing truant from the chamber music classes and leaving when he was 13. Vecsey was under Hubay by the age of eight, had left by the time he was 10 and barely had time for a couple of years' further study with Joachim before beginning his career. Relating Lasserson to fellow Auer pupils, he was one year younger than Efrem Zimbalist and one year older than Mischa Elman. Zimbalist started studying with Auer at 12 and, at 18, was away with a Gold Medal to earn his living. Elman was just turning 12 when he started studying with Auer and he had no formal training after the age of 14. Lasserson's close contemporary, Kathleen Parlow, who went to Auer when she was 15, was on her own by the time she turned 18. Even a comparatively slow starter such as Emil Telmányi, who was 13 when he went to Hubay and took his studies very seriously, was 'in career' by the age of 19.

So we have the picture of Sascha Lasserson as a serious student, quite a high-flier but not one of Auer's wunderkind favourites – and in no hurry to finish his studies. It would seem that his parents had enough money to support him while he got a good grounding; perhaps his father, L'vov, who was a violinist, was able to find work in St Petersburg. The most important factor was that they did not exploit him for financial gain, as the parents of so many brilliant young fiddlers did. Lasserson senior was Sascha's first teacher. "I wanted to learn," Lasserson said in a 1956 interview. "My earliest memories are of fiddles. My father had a number attached by pegs to the walls of his study and as a child I spent hours just gazing at them. Everything about them fascinated me. I liked their colour, their shape. I wanted to handle them. It was natural that I should want to play." The boy began lessons at 5 and must have made astonishing progress, because when he was 10 he played Spohr's Ninth Concerto in Helsingfors under the great Finnish conductor and composer Robert Kajanus. That year, 1900, he was also accepted into Nikolai Galkin's class at the Imperial Conservatory. Jews were forbidden to live in St Petersburg unless they converted to Christianity, but allowance was made for extraordinary talents and in such cases the parents, too, were often permitted to stay in the city. The Conservatory was presided over by Glazunov who, despite his propensity for alcohol, was an excellent principal. Galkin, then in his mid-40s, was Auer's pupil and former assistant but was himself one of Russia's outstanding violinists, having studied with Joachim, Sauret and Wieniawski after leaving Auer. He had a second career as a conductor, having run the orchestra at the Conservatory and taken the conducting class there since 1890. He was musical director of the Alexander Theatre and was also in charge of the symphony concerts at Pavlovsk, so he was a fine all-round musician. He had been a full professor of violin since 1892 and some of his students stayed the whole course with him.

The Russian school of violin playing was something of a melting pot, absorbing much of its strength from the traditional centres of fiddling in central Europe. Auer was a Hungarian and many Czech players had contributed to the mix, including the Hrimaly brothers and Laub. It was hearing the greatest Czech virtuoso of the time, František Ondrícek, in his home town of Vitebsk that inspired the young Lasserson to study the violin with all his might. Two of the outstanding string players whom the boy would have heard in St Petersburg were of Polish extraction: the cellist Alexander Wierzbilowicz, who played in a celebrity trio with Auer and the pianist Annette Essipova, and the violinist Karol Grigorowicz. The latter was, to judge from his pitifully few recordings, easily the finest fiddler in Russia. He led the ensemble which toured the world as the St Petersburg Quartet – at home it was known as the Duke of Mecklenburg's Quartet. He was also a superb soloist in the late 19th-century style, making use of much portamento but very little vibrato. Grigorowicz's beautiful tone, aristocratic bowing and matchless left-hand technique set the standard; but of course Auer himself was still a wonderful artist whose style was more vulnerable but probably all the more affecting for that.

In 1902, after 18 months with Galkin, Sascha Lasserson transferred to Auer's class, a large – rather too large – assembly of some of the best violin students in the Russian empire. All were boys. Parlow, the first foreigner and first girl to be admitted, left a vivid account of what it was like in 1906, when she arrived: "On entering the classroom I found it filled to overflowing with teenage boys. Afterwards I found the class numbered 45. Auer introduced me, whereupon they rose and applauded. [...] Two boys played before I was called – Efrem Zimbalist and Josef Piastro. I had to play the Bach Fugue in G minor and the Paganini Concerto. From then on I had two 40-minute lessons a week. The others, when they saw fit to appear, had 15 or 20 minutes once a week. One day a week we had a two-hour quartet session." Parlow, who herself skimped on her second instrument, the piano, hinted at a certain amount of indiscipline and slacking. Nevertheless, most of her impressions were positive: "The joy I had in my lessons is hard to describe. First there was the preparation for the lessons themselves and then listening to that remarkable class with the aptitude for the violin one and all showed. [...] During the winter practically the entire violin repertoire was covered, and I sat in that room twice a week from 2.00 until 6.00 and drank it all in, coming away utterly exhausted but happy, and how much I learned from hearing all those lessons! [...] The whole system of the Conservatory seemed to me (and still does) to be ideal. The students received a good high-school education, but with sufficient time to practise their instruments. [...] the students had to play a recital at least once a month. There were two student recitals a week and it was obligatory for the pupils to attend all recitals."

Much of the learning process, then, consisted of hearing your peers play. And Lasserson was fortunate enough to be in on the one-man revolution that changed the sound of the violin for ever. It was, in any case, a time of rapid change in violin playing, with Fritz Kreisler embodying a new technique of constant vibrato, virtually overlapping from note to note. But no one could have foreseen the emergence of Mischa Elman. Though taught from the age of four by his father, Elman always claimed to have been most influenced by the sound made by his grandfather, a klezmer fiddler. What he often omitted to mention in later life – but revealed in a 1904 interview – was that he never actually heard his grandfather; he absorbed the sound at second hand from a gipsy who had often heard his grandfather play. The Elman tone was probably present in its essentials very early, as a wealthy countess offered to sponsor Mischa when he was five (his father refused, as conversion was a condition of the sponsorship). The writer Henry Roth was surely right in suggesting that when Auer first heard Elman, he had never previously encountered such a sound – and that the boy influenced the master almost as much as the master the boy! Be that as it may, the 16 months that Elman spent in Auer's class in 1903 and 1904 had an electrifying effect on the other students; and Elman's subsequent immediate success as a concert prodigy precipitated a stampede of hopeful young Jewish violinists from the ghettos and the Pale of Settlement. Sascha Lasserson was very friendly with Elman; they shared a wealthy patron, who gave each of them a fine violin, but they were totally different as boys and as artists. The story goes that, when staying with their patron, they both went off to practise. Lasserson duly ran through all the scales and exercises prescribed by Auer, but in the pauses between he could hear Elman playing all manner of excerpts of repertoire – and no scales.

Auer was clearly a superb teacher who managed to bring out the best in his pupils without affecting their individuality. "My pupils must express themselves," he would say. "Each pupil has his own inborn aptitudes, his own personal qualities as regards tone and interpretation. I always have made an individual study of each pupil, and given each pupil individual treatment. And always, always I have encouraged them to develop freely in their own way as regards inspiration and ideals, so long as this was not contrary to aesthetic principles and those of my art. My idea has always been to help bring out what nature has already given, rather than to use dogma to force a student's natural inclinations into channels I myself might prefer." No two alumni of his class sounded alike and a number of them became major personalities of the violin. Parlow used to say that Auer was successful because he had the best students in the first place; but you cannot gainsay his success rate. Nor did he destroy pupils, as Carl Flesch sometimes did, although he could be very demanding and even irascible – he once threw an ashtray at Myron Polyakin, who was being particularly argumentative. "Another great principle in my teaching, one which is productive of results," Auer told Frederick H Martens, "is to demand as much as possible of the pupil. Then he will give you something!" He had the knack of encouraging all his students to achieve a good vibrato – consider the contrast with Hubay, who bequeathed all his pupils a wide, almost 'wah-wah' style of vibrato. On the other hand, Auer was no more helpful to his students on technical matters than was Joachim: they either worked things out on their own or asked one of his assistants, such as the Armenian teacher Ioannes Nalbandyan. However, Auer was very critical if anyone fell down technically. "Auer wanted result," said Lasserson. "How that result was obtained was secondary, bearing in mind, however, that the pupils were, in the main, technically extraordinary. Auer allowed free scope to the individual. He never taught vibrato. It was there. If anything was wrong he corrected it. Otherwise Auer never altered anything merely for the sake of altering. He allowed each pupil to work out his own particular identity; to become, as it were, the perfect blueprint of himself. Auer was not concerned with producing automata, but artists by right of personality. The Auer pupil bears a hallmark only in that members of the same family, conserving their individuality, yet maintain the family likeness. Auer never taught technique in the accepted sense. He taught music."

When it came to the all-important daily practice, Auer took a typically pragmatic line. "Practice should represent the utmost concentration," he said. "It is better to play with concentration for two hours than to practise eight without. I should say that four hours would be a good maximum practice time – I never ask more of my pupils – and that during each minute of the time the brain be as active as the fingers." Auer's forté was perhaps his acute ear for a pupil's inherent strengths so that the weaknesses became less apparent. In Lasserson's case he may well have sensed that, for all his violinistic skill – which saw him play two major concerto performances in St Petersburg, the Vieuxtemps Fifth under Kajanus and the Glazunov under the composer's own baton – this particular young man did not have the temperament for a solo career. He may even have guessed that Lasserson's analytical mind and fascination with the mechanics of violin playing would make him an ideal teacher.

As to repertoire, Auer himself told us (in *Violin Playing As I Teach It*) the sort of things he liked his students to cut their teeth on. He swore by Kreutzer's 40 Etudes and Rode's 24 Caprices as foundations of technique. Then came such teaching concertos as the Viotti A minor, the Rode A minor and E minor, the Kreutzer D minor and D major, and the early Spohr D minor (No.2), as well as such Vieuxtemps pieces as *Rêverie*, the *Morceau de Salon* in D minor, *Ballade et Polonaise, Tarantelle* and even the *Fantasie Appassionata*. Then came the Rode and Rovelli Etudes and the 24 Caprices by Auer's own teacher Dont, as well as Spohr's Seventh, Eighth, Ninth and Eleventh concertos and pieces by Wieniawski: the *Légende*, some of the mazurkas, perhaps the A major *Polonaise*. At this stage he also recommended Sarasate's *Spanish Dances* and the transcriptions of Chopin *Nocturnes* by Sarasate, Wilhelmj, and himself. With the Rode and Dont Caprices truly mastered, the student could move on to the core concertos of Beethoven (including the *Romances*), Mendelssohn, Brahms, Bruch. Lalo (the *Symphonie Espagnole*), Saint-Saëns and Tchaikovsky. Auer required pupils to play a complete Bach solo sonata or partita for their graduation examinations – Lasserson won his Gold Medal with the D minor Partita – but used only certain movements of solo Bach for teaching and did not think much of the Bach concertos, apart from their slow movements. Instead he favoured transcriptions (not realising that many of Kreisler's were actually that master's own compositions) and such fare as Ries's *Third Suite*. Later he would add pieces by his own pupils, Zimbalist and Achron, to the list.

The Auer pupil then proceeded to baroque sonatas by Tartini and others, as well as the concertos of Vieuxtemps, Wieniawski, Ernst and Paganini – Auer took much of the latter's output very seriously and made an interesting edition of the 24th Caprice with piano accompaniment. Another of his war-horses, a severe test of bow control, was the Paganini *Perpetuum Mobile*; and he advocated the learning of virtuoso pieces by Ernst and others. But Auer also laid great stress on a good cantabile and recommended many pieces for developing that art, for instance the Bach-Wilhelmj *Air on the G String*. He encouraged study of all the major violin works by Mozart, all ten sonatas by Beethoven, all three by Brahms and selected pieces by Schumann. Students also emerged from his class with a good deal of Russian music under their belts – soon after coming to Britain, Sascha Lasserson was able to give the local première of the Conus Concerto. The violin repertoire was much more circumscribed then than it is now, but Auer's taste was generally sound. Of course, pupils were on a good wicket if they played his editions – even more if they mastered his cadenzas into the bargain – and no one today would countenance the changes he inflicted on many masterpieces; but by the standards of the time he was relatively conservative in his editing.

Auer was also particularly helpful to his students when they were trying to launch their careers. He always had a wealth of advice for them concerning business matters and he usually weighed in with contacts and letters of recommendation to help them get work. Even when they were launched in the profession they were encouraged to come back for advice. In all, Sascha Lasserson was in Leopold Auer's orbit for 14 years and he always made it clear that, in his opinion, he could not have had a better teacher.

Tully Potter is a music journalist with a particular interest in performing practice as revealed in historic recordings. He is a frequent contributor to 'The Strad', and is the editor of 'Classic Record Collector'. He has written a biography of Adolph Busch, and has a book on the great string quartet ensembles in preparation.

Reminiscenses of Sascha

Martin Bainbridge

I was privileged to study with Sascha Lasserson from 1959, when I was sixteen years old, and I continued with him for six years. My first recollection of Sascha was when my father, a session musician at that time, took me to play for him, on the strong recommendation of his colleagues Anthony Gilbert, David McCallum and others, who insisted that Sascha Lasserson was the only choice of teacher in this country, such was his fabulous reputation.

Having been a Junior at the Royal Academy since the age of eleven, my first meeting with the great man at his Queensborough Terrace studio was quite a daunting experience. After hearing me play he was very encouraging, and suggested I should have six lessons to see how we got on; I stayed with him for six years! I soon realised how little I understood about good violin playing, but I did work very hard on Kreutzer, Dont, scales and, of course, unaccompanied Bach.

He was such an inspiration, and always so encouraging, coaxing me through the early stages with such expertise and understanding. Very often after my lesson, if no other pupil followed, he would play. Everything he played was made in heaven, and his unaccompanied Bach was the most moving experience I could imagine.

I can see him now; the vision is still vivid in my mind, forty years on, his Player's No 3 cigarette angled over the right 'f' hole, with what appeared to be two inches of burnt ash miraculously staying in place!

He had wonderful tales of players past and present. He could demonstrate, with such ease, their various weaknesses and strengths. I remember the great excitement of seeing the 'star' players of the day, such as Elizabeth Matesky and Tessa Robbins, to name but a few, arrive at the studio for their lessons. He treated everybody in the same way, with great respect and warmth, and he was always eager to show off a pupil's particular strengths.

He had a great sense of humour, with a wealth of fascinating stories, such as that of the American violinist who phoned him from America requesting a lesson, which was duly arranged. He arrived at the studio, got his fiddle out, put the middle movement of the Saint-Saens B minor concerto on the stand and asked a very surprised Sascha how to play the harmonics at the end of the movement. Once Sascha demonstrated and explained it to him, he proceeded to put his fiddle away and promptly departed, never to be seen again!

I am so pleased at the efforts to make sure that this great artist and teacher's name will live on. It has greatly saddened me in recent years that Sascha Lasserson, a truly great violinist and remarkable teacher, never got the true recognition he richly deserved in his lifetime.

I have been teaching in the north of England for many years. I really try my utmost to impart some of the knowledge and understanding Sascha Lasserson bestowed, to some extent, on myself.

I consider myself highly privileged to call myself a Lasserson pupil, and I believe having studied with Sascha Lasserson was one of the most important and unforgettable experiences in my life.

Martin Bainbridge studied with Sascha Lasserson for six years before entering the London orchestral scene. He played in the LPO and the BBC Symphony Orchestra, as well as freelancing, before moving north to establish his own teaching practice. He is Head of Strings at Yarm School.

David Bateman

To start at the end: I last met Sascha Lasserson by chance outside Bunty Lempfert's studio at Shepherd's Bush a year or so before he died. He appeared so extraordinarily pleased to see me as, of course, I was to see him again after many years. Yet I thought after so long I'd just be a very vague memory – one of the many British orchestral violinists and teachers to whom he'd given his invaluable help and who, in comparison to the dedicated violinists he'd worked with and taught during his life in Russia (not to mention far better known ones in Britain), I'd have hardly rated to activate his memory. But there he was, beaming with happiness, a shy, deeply caring greeting, with his wonderful domed head and twinkling grey Russian eyes behind thick pebble glasses, dressed as ever in a formal dark suit and with the ever-present cigarette. It is reported that one day he lit one, then played through Paganini's *Moto Perpetuo* – including its repeat, enabling the cigarette to be removed at its conclusion, just before it would have burnt his lips on the very next beat!

It was during my 18-month period of National Service in the string section of the RAF Central Band at Uxbridge when I first heard of Sascha Lasserson. By then I'd studied for three years at the Royal Academy of Music. Several of my talented National Service violinist colleagues talked about his excellence and, in two cases, spoke of their own fathers' admiration for him, being old time professionals. He was spoken of as 'the professional's coach and teacher'. So I decided to try and have lessons from him, if he'd take me on.

Up to that time I'd been trained in the Rowsby Woof and Rostal methods, in each case 'once removed'. Sascha Lasserson was known to coach well-known quartet leaders and soloists, and I also learnt in conversations about him that he'd played the

Glazunov Concerto under the composer's baton in Russia, could play all kinds of fiendishly difficult concertos by Ernst and Vieuxtemps that were by then rarely heard, and of course more current repertoire; the Paganini concertos, the Prokofievs and the Walton, not to mention caprices, studies and spectacular solos. He had authoritative alternative editings of sections of the Tchaikovsky, and was wonderfully sympathetic as a teacher of Bach unaccompanied sonatas. Still more incredibly, at the other end of the spectrum, in but twelve lessons he would guarantee to teach – from scratch – professional musicians of other instruments, sufficiently well to enable them to play the violin in pit orchestras and for the silent films! That was at a time when 'doubling' was literally another string to one's bow, giving added job security and earning power. I wonder whether those two expressions 'from scratch' and 'more strings to one's bow' could have originated from violin tuition?

Seriously though, I realised that I was about to have lessons with a very great teacher and went to him for a first trial lesson, hoping so much that he would accept me. This lesson took place at 60 St Quintin Avenue, W10. Like most 'first times', one is particularly alert and strung up. Everything on that occasion made a very strong impression: the Edwardian style and feel of the room; photos of his distinguished Russian fellow pupils and colleagues of that doyen of teachers, Leopold Auer; a photo of Heifetz, with the inscription 'from Jascha to Sascha'; and those of Zimbalist, Milstein and Elman – formidable colleagues indeed! Not a little overwhelming, yet not so much that I wasn't keenly aware of the way in which he gave me those never-to-be-forgotten instructions in his kind but clear and authoritative way on how to hold the bow and instrument. He demonstrated the reasons why it would work better to adopt that extra pronation of the forearm and fingers of the Russian School, rather than continue to use my Anglo-French bow-hold. The Russian offers a far greater degree of control and the ability for quicker detaché strokes at any dynamic – in fact, a way of performing all bowing needs without necessitating a change in one's bow-hold at all, save perhaps for that of up and down-bow staccato. What a vitally important lesson it was – one that my own pupils would later benefit from, not to mention a few professional colleagues who suffered from attacks of the 'pearlies' (bow-wobble) from time to time, or had difficulty with spiccato or sautillé bowing.

During my initial playing to him, he quickly saw that my left hand was not consistently aligned with the fingerboard in the lower positions. In a single re-adjustment he cured my worst and most infuriating problem, namely the inconsistent spacing between fingers on different days, depending at what angle they approached the strings (a small difference of angle makes a terrific difference to that spaced feel). But with his method, the index finger is always lightly touching the neck with the root line of that finger at the top of the fingerboard for the first four or five positions; I never looked back. At last! I had the simple solution for that mysterious inconsistency of mechanically produced 'variable' intonation that I'd suffered from, which meant that one day's careful intonation practice didn't bring commensurate rewards on another day. He also pointed out the importance of approaching each string with as consistent a hand alignment as possible, by moving the left elbow under the violin clearly for each string change.

Mr Lasserson was very kind in supporting pupils' concerts, and when one of the great Russian soloists visited London, he would take a pupil along and sometimes introduce them. So it was on one special occasion that Norman Nelson (who played at one time or other in the front desk positions of most London orchestras and who later went on to lead in Vancouver both the orchestra and chamber ensembles there) was taken to meet the superlative but formidable Heifetz – Norman's hero. The great man was charming to him and agreed to give his autograph, only for that charm to be turned into icy fury, hissing "I can't sign THAT," when Norman, after fumbling to find a worthy page for it, offered the hard-backed book he was carrying under his arm and whose title he'd momentarily forgotten. It turned out to be Karl Marx's Das Kapital!

I remember Mr Lasserson telling me how he went along with another pupil to help translate for David Oistrakh when he first played with the BBC orchestra at the Maida Vale Studio 1. After the rehearsal he took that pupil back to meet Oistrakh, joined by some of his other pupils – players in the orchestra – and persuaded him to play some unaccompanied Bach, which I gathered was, from his teaching advice later, critically revealing and possibly highlighted differences of approach from the Auer school of his day.

At lessons he would sometimes talk about Auer's despotic approach to the young Jewish prodigies, whose families could only remain in St Petersburg if their sons worked hard enough to please the teacher's rigorous standards. Auer would hand out almost impossibly demanding projects each week – say, a concerto, a caprice, a couple of studies, unaccompanied Bach, a solo piece, and maybe an accompanied sonata; anyhow, too much to be able to do. Something had to be omitted; and thus a dangerous gamble was embarked upon. As the pupil came into the room, Auer would closely watch him unpack and tune, and then invariably ask for the one piece that he'd not done ... out of the room he'd then be summarily sent! If that was repeated too often, the whole family, as Jews, would have to leave the city, as their child would no longer be officially studying at the Conservatoire. Whilst Auer was a stickler for pupils accurately following his edited instructions, Mr Lasserson said he would often not follow his own bowings and fingerings playing chamber music.

Although obviously of a different school, Mr Lasserson had tremendous admiration for Kreisler but not so much for some of our own leading players who, he implied, hadn't the kind of belcanto 'authentic' playing that he liked. Here I sometimes disagreed with him, and truthfully found some of his backward slides – typical of a style one can hear in recordings of groups like the Lener Quartet – almost distasteful, in contrast to the clean, beautiful playing of the likes of Eli Goren or Norbert Brainin. Yet as I say that, I could sense, in spite of my preference for more modern, cleaner shifts, that when he picked up his Spiritus Sorsana violin to demonstrate, a door opened to a by-gone age of fine, poignant playing, now only heard on very old recordings by the likes of Ysaye, Kubelik, Hubay and, in this country, Albert Sammons.

One of the amazing technical features of his left-hand playing was the strangely leisurely way in which his fingers apparently moved, keeping so close to the strings, while the overall tempo was actually very fast. I well remember his playing of the last movement of the Mendelssohn, where he avoided the usual paired semiquaver bumps, but rather demonstrated its likeness to the Scherzo from the *Midsummer Night's Dream* with longer phrasing. Then there was his advice at the beginning of the first movement to do the slightly gulpy printed bowing and NOT smooth it out; this gives it a quite different sense of youthful urgency.

Paradoxically, it was the way in which he imparted his musical convictions in a clear yet undogmatic way that helped to show a work's possibilities and assisted me eventually to come to my own interpretation. It so helps to be given a firm tradition from which to develop – and sometimes even from which to move away.

I would now like to mention here an invaluable little exercise which I suspect he gave to most pupils along with broken thirds. This one needs to be played softly with NO VIBRATO and using a beautifully balanced bow. For it is mostly on two strings, playing fourths resolving to thirds (apart from the linking slides between 3rd and 1st positions made with the 2nd finger), indicating clearly the shifts up and down between string changes and played over two octaves in C major. This exercise is good for refining (all together) one's 'ear', the right and left hand, with the latter using the very subtlest finger-tip adjustments for fine tuning; after all, perfect fourths have to be just that!

He used to say that the most important role for a teacher was 'to be another pair of ears'. But I would say his greatest gift was his love and skill of teaching with his ability to adapt to the needs and nature of each pupil's character, almost obliquely overcoming their weaknesses while never belittling them. As another pupil friend said, "He made it strangely possible to approach the most difficult music with confidence."

He had some brilliant adaptations of important Kreutzer studies. Then there was the way in which he would sometimes ask for a study or caprice to be played at an unexpectedly slow pace from that which one had reached in practice, thus breaking up one's habitual feel for its sequences. This sometimes had the rather dire effect of leaving one standing embarrassedly amidst a pile of damaged and blundered-upon notes ... after which, with a little smile, he'd make the telling observation, "You see? Any fool can play fast, but not any fool can play slowly."

Whenever I go to pick up the Glazunov concerto again, I can hear so clearly his strong Russian accent saying of its first theme, "It is the sadness of the Russian people." He knew of that only too well.

David Bateman began violin studies as a schoolboy in Luton with Leslie Dawson, before moving to the RAM to study with Robert Masters (with horn as second study under Aubrey Brain). He went on to study with Sascha Lasserson during and after National Service. He has freelanced with almost all London's Symphony and Chamber Orchestras, particularly with the RPO during Beecham's last two years, was Head of Strings at Oundle for ten years and also taught at Harrow and Eton — without either knowing his connection with the other!

Lionel Bentley

How did I first hear of Sascha Lasserson? As a teenager I was playing in J. Lyons' Coventry Street 'Corner House', earning £4.16s for a seven-day week. In those days J. Lyons employed small orchestras in all their West End restaurants and they were enormously popular with the customers. The type of music varied considerably from a modest trio to groups of fourteen or more, playing anything from classical (not much of this) to jazz with, sometimes, a singer. Popular light music was the norm and several famous players were to be heard in the top restaurants, notably Albert Sandler in the Trocadero (long since gone), Daisy Kennedy and 'Jack' Jacobs. I was fortunate to join a group of eleven players directed by a very good violinist named Max Roitt, who took an interest in me.

Occasionally a little man, a Mr Bloch, would appear at the back of the platform offering strings for sale; a useful contact for us. One day he asked me who was my teacher. I had not studied seriously for about a year because of my need to earn a living, and I told him that I really needed a good teacher. He said, "Well, you know who to go to, don't you?" No, I said. "Why, Lasserson, of course!" He pronounced his name 'Larzerson'. I said that I had not heard of him. He looked hard at me and said, "You go to him".

I made enquiries and found that Sascha had only recently come to England. He had been a distinguished pupil of Leopold Auer in Russia and was living and teaching in a large house in St Quintin Avenue, North Kensington.

I arranged to meet and play to him, and went along wondering what was in store for me. I was soon to know. Pupils waited for their lesson in a room adjoining his teaching room and could hear the previous pupil playing. This one was studying Tartini's *Devil's Trill* sonata and I was suitably humbled by the time I went in to play. He agreed to accept me despite my shattered nerves, and a weekly one-hour lesson was settled at a fee of half a guinea, a sum not too easy to find in those hard-up days.

From that day my ideas of violin playing altered considerably; first of all my bow arm. I had been taught the old Joachim style with a dropped right arm and a high wrist. This was quickly dealt with and we continued with scales and studies before embarking upon repertoire.

I was always intrigued by the attractive sound which he produced and which he maintained to the end of his life. It is useless, of course, to try to copy a sound. It is much too individual. Nevertheless, listening to a tone quality that pleases can influence one's own approach to this all-important matter, vibrato being only one of several factors requiring careful study. His methods of fingering and bowing were always sound and practical, comparing favourably with many modern editings.

After some time in St Quintin Avenue, teaching was continued in a fine and well-equipped studio in Finchley Road, St John's Wood, London, where he not only taught his pupils but held pupils' concerts (a nerve-wracking experience) and, on one memorable occasion, gave a recital himself, the programme including a Paganini caprice. He also gave a splendid live broadcast of Beethoven sonatas with which I was much impressed. How many people would remember those momentous days, I wonder?

He smoked constantly during a lesson even while he was playing, the ash from his cigarette growing longer and longer until it seemed about to drop onto the violin. It never did, but I was always worried that it might. He never taught beginners but would accept a pupil who showed promise, correct any obvious faults and, when these were satisfactorily dealt with, go right on from there.

His interpretation of the Bach unaccompanied sonatas was remarkably clear and incisive. He did not play the four-note chords starting from the top note as we so often hear them (an unsatisfactory way to play chords, anyway) but included the bottom note in a way that was logical and musically convincing. I always envied his up and down-bow staccato bowing, and his double-stop trills were a delight to the ear. An occasional anecdote of the Auer Class, when Heifetz (a fellow student) and others would perform, gave one's lesson a more than usual interest. Kreisler and Heifetz were his idols and he often mentioned Erica Morini, a violinist he much admired.

Sascha Lasserson was a modest and loveable man, a great teacher, always encouraging and constructive while maintaining the traditions and prestige of the incomparable Leopold Auer School.

Lionel Bentley began his career as a teenager by playing in silent films and the theatre, during which time he began studies with Sascha Lasserson. Subsequently he played at Covent Garden under Bruno Walter and Tullio Serafin. He was co-leader of the LSO and RPO, led the Boyd Neel and London Chamber orchestras, was Professor at RAM for fourteen years, and also taught at Eton College for thirteen years. He spent four years in RAF Signals during the war, when he did not play at all.

Yvonne Bowness

For a number of years I had lessons with Albert Sammons, both at College and privately. Albert was a very dear and kindly tutor, who moulded one's playing to give maximum feeling. My first lesson with Sascha was rather a shock. Scales!! For six weeks I had to play just thirds with the left thumb away from the neck of the violin. I found this rather shattering, but intonation and finger power were much improved. After this, another shock – the Viotti concerto.

One is bound to remember Sascha's flat, his perpetual cigarette and his continual search for perfection. I had to end my lessons earlier than I had hoped, as my family arrived and for a time required my attention.

Since then I have been occupied with family, pupils, and freelance playing. I have always felt that one should try to pass on to future generations the wonderful teaching we experienced. Many pupils nowadays will not accept the regime given to us, but the love and enjoyment of music must continue.

Yvonne Bowness studied with Dorothy Walenn while at school, and then with Albert Sammons at the RCM. Later, on the advice of her sister, the cellist Joy Hall, she went to Sascha Lasserson in the mid-1940s. She has worked as a freelance, and for many years has taught violin and viola at Kimbolton School.

Jimmy Brown

I first heard of Sascha through a friend, Ron Macaulay. At the time we were both saxophone players with the Ken Mackintosh Band. We both played the violin 'passably', but wanted to progress. We heard that Sascha was a fine teacher, and we both had lessons with him for several months. This helped me to pass the audition to enter Trinity College of Music, where I studied for three years – the first with Oscar Rosen, and the last two with Nicholas Roth.

I can't remember the actual year I was with Sascha – maybe 1960 – but I do remember that the lessons took place in a studio in Queensway. I remember being given an ear test before he would accept me; a three octave scale – is it sharp at the top? Flat at the bottom? I think he didn't want to waste his time.

Sascha always had a cigarette in his mouth, even while playing. We used to have many a laugh, and the lessons were most enjoyable. I don't think he knew what to make of me – a saxophone / flute / clarinet player in a dance band being so keen on the violin. He used to say that English players were very talented. They were taught to put their fingers in the right place but – unfortunately – were not taught to listen. I can recall him talking about two of his pupils, Max Jaffa and Tessa Robbins.

I can also recall Sascha walking round the room playing The Bee, which he did quite often. He always stressed the importance of practising slowly, saying that a good study to practise was the Kreutzer No.8, and that scales must never be forgotten.

I have very good memories of Sascha's sense of humour and teaching skills. He was one of life's gentlemen.

Jimmy Brown studied with Sascha Lasserson while working as a multi-instrumentalist dance-band musician, subsequently continuing his studies at Trinity College.

Averil Carmalt

I studied with Mr Lasserson from about 1965 until the time of his death. I was already playing for my living then, and my lessons were often sporadic, but I shall never forget my elation – and the sense of honour – when Mr Lasserson said he would take me on as a pupil. Though his command of English was of course rather limited (on the bow "the thumb should be 'opposight' the middle finger, isn't it?") it delighted me; he could convey exactly what he wanted by just being who he was. We learned volumes on some upper wavelength not limited by words, and his brilliant diagnosis of one's hang-ups, difficulties, phobias put one in mind of the best kind of wonderful doctor. Mr Lasserson could put his finger on the spot and unravel technical problems which had bugged one for years. Difficulties melted away in a few minutes. This was perhaps his greatest and quite uncanny gift as a teacher. But he was also clear-seeing to an incredible degree, with a degree of utter truthfulness that was unnerving at times. A man rather too honest and straight for the musical profession as it is, I think? Perhaps this was the reason Mr Lasserson had far less than his fair share of fame and success in the worldly sense. Perhaps it doesn't matter now, for he lives on in the hearts of so many of us, and we are eternally grateful to him.

He kept up his own playing right to the end of his life in a way that very few people do – delighting us with fearsomely difficult passages, brilliantly executed, at the age of 86 or 88, and totally magic interpretations of unaccompanied Bach. Always stylistically pure, always authentic in content, yet totally individual, conveying at first hand the tone, meaning and atmosphere of Bach – it could have been Bach himself playing. What a privilege that was to share, and what a memory to treasure.

Our lessons were formal and Mr Lasserson never wasted time,

yet there were some wonderful stories: the amateur who came to him for a lesson, bringing no music to play, so Mr Lasserson asked for a scale and the man slid up and down the string on one finger. "No," said Mr Lasserson, "you use the fingers one after the other." "Are you sure?" asked the man – greatly to Mr Lasserson's and our delight.

There is a rather tricky run at the end of the cadenza to the first movement of the Vieuxtemps A Minor Concerto – Mr Lasserson used to delight in saying how it worried well-known players – Elman, Zimbalist, Heifetz, etc. – "and my pupils when I ask them to play it, they shake, they shake! Now play it!" by which time I was laughing so much that it came off fairly well.

Others will tell of Mr Lasserson's efforts, in his early days as an unknown in this country, to get work done on his violin at Hill's. After several abortive efforts he gave up and asked, instead, to try some violins. This, Hill's were eager to comply with – whereupon Mr Lasserson shut the door of the room they showed him into, and played ALL the Bach unaccompanied sonatas one after the other. At the end of what must have been hours, Messrs Hills' reaction was "Yes, Mr Lasserson" to anything he wanted.

I don't think any of his pupils will expect to see that depth of wisdom and experience again nor, as I can testify, his wonderful compassion, patience and encouragement of the untalented. He, who had known the greatest players, gave all he had for the least of us. His humility, complete lack of self-advertisement, total genuineness, shone like a beacon in a world of egoists and exhibitionists. Though small in stature, he towered over us all in real terms. We still talk about him and I do hope that – somehow – he knows how great is our gratitude and how we love him.

Averil Carmalt was a pupil of Sascha Lasserson from 1964 until his death. Since then she has divided her time between freelance orchestral work, examining, and teaching – keeping as much time as possible for sonata work and chamber music.

(See the Appendix for Sascha's exercises for warming up and flexibility, and independence of fingers, contributed by Miss Carmalt)

Desmond Cecil CMG

My memories of Sascha Lasserson derive from a brief period of a few months in 1964-65, but nevertheless have stayed extremely vivid over the years. At the time I was reading PPE at Oxford University and had already arranged to study with Max Rostal in Switzerland. I subsequently had five happy years as a musician in Switzerland, before switching to the world of diplomacy – while remaining an avid chamber musician.

A university violinist colleague, who was a friend of Elisabeth Matesky, recommended that I should have a few lessons with Sascha in London before I moved to Switzerland. This was one of the better recommendations which I have been given in my life. From our first meeting in his West London flat I was captivated with Sascha. As one got to know this apparently quiet, unassuming little man, one realised the immense depths of his violinistic, musical and human personality. As a fiddle teacher he was perceptive, sympathetic and wise. He immediately spotted his pupils' deficiencies and took enormous pains to explain these in ways which built up rather than belittled their confidence. A lesser teacher would have taken an easier critical path. Sascha tried to use his pupils' strong points, which even the least talented possess, as vehicles for correction of their weak points. While never allowing faults to be overlooked he made one feel that, even when beset with technical and musical problems, there was always a logical route forward. He would give a quiet and simple word of advice, and suddenly a problem would be put into perspective.

The violinistic side of the lessons was highlighted by fascinating musical insights. Here was a man who had known and played with so many of the Russian greats – Auer, Heifetz, Elman, and Glazunov among many others. In the middle of a lesson, he would modestly let slip a casual remark about how Glazunov had conducted him in a performance of the violin concerto, or of how Heifetz had tackled a particularly tricky corner. For those who were ready to listen, these remarks were worth their weight in gold.

There was also the generous human side of the man. In an increasingly commercial age, here was a man who often set aside extra time for his pupils – without extra charge. The lessons ended, not when the clock reached the appointed hour, but when the right violinistic and musical results had been achieved. If he never accumulated the worldly wealth that some of his more materialistic colleagues did, he accumulated spiritual wealth in the memories and affection of his many pupils. This was his well-deserved reward for a richly fulfilled life.

Nearly thirty-five years on from my brief encounter with Sascha, while deep in some chamber music session, I still think of wise advice that Sascha gave me and am reminded of the ever-courteous and sympathetic manner in which this advice was given. Such memories are rare and to be treasured in life.

Desmond Cecil studied with Sascha Lasserson before leading a Swiss chamber orchestar for five years. He switched to Diplomacy, serving in several European capitals until retirement in 1995. Subsequently he was involved with nuclear environmental clean-up in Russia. He is a member of the Board of the Royal Philharmonic Society and of the Jupiter Orchestra. He remains an enthusiastic chamber musician.

Marie Clements

When I left the Royal Academy I was unhappy with my playing. I had facility, but felt that I did not understand how I played. It was, indeed, all imitation rather than understanding, and I entered a period of deep dissatisfaction. This lasted until a friend in a quartet advised me to approach Sascha Lasserson for lessons. She gave me his telephone number, and bullied me until I actually rang him. My debt to her is one that I can never repay.

Sascha agreed to see me, and off I went to his Shepherds Bush studio. The door was opened by a little man peering up at me (I am quite tall). I played to him in his crowded and untidy room, and he agreed to take me as a pupil. The first few weeks were spent trying to understand what he was saying, and I was never able to understand how he retained such a strong accent.

Then the magic started, as he opened up for me a world of possibilities based on understanding. There was no problem he could not solve and, as time went on, this lovely funny man became increasingly precious to me. He always encouraged, only getting irritated if he felt that you had not worked, and I cannot forget him saying to me, "Don't be upset! I know you have worked, let's do it again."

I loved my lessons, and I worked hard. We would occasionally break for a cigarette, for I also smoked in those days. Sascha would say, "You shouldn't smoke, it's bad for your bowing arm. At least, don't do it on concert days!"

He would reminisce about his lessons in Russia and about travelling with Glazunov ("He was a poor pianist"!). He would play Ernst's *Last Rose of Summer* and Bruch's *Scottish Fantasy*, which were hair-raisingly difficult and not often heard. His technique was phenomenal, and his joy in playing was infectious.

When it came to his birthday he would say in mock surprise,

"What makes people think I would like cigarettes and brandy?"

That little man, with his poor sight and thick glasses, and amazing personality, will stay with me forever.

Some of us, if we are lucky, may meet one or two people who affect the rest of our lives. For me, Sascha was the one.

Marie Clements studied at the RAM for three years where she did a Performers' Course. She was a pupil of Sascha Lasserson for six years from 1968.

Harold Colman

I had my first lesson with Mr Lasserson in October 1947. I had travelled down from Northampton, and I remember playing the first movement of the Bruch G Minor Concerto as an audition piece. I was accepted as a pupil, and advised to start work on the Dont 24 Caprices. I went for a lesson every two weeks, and Mr Lasserson's fee was two guineas but, because I was a young professional, he reduced it to one guinea.

We worked on the Spohr No. 9 concerto, Vieuxtemps Nos. 2 and 5 concertos, Mendelssohn, Beethoven, Tchaikovsky concertos; Lalo *Symphonie Espagnole* – and he would demonstrate the most difficult passages with perfect intonation and accuracy.

He never used a shoulder rest. His shaped staccato was a joy to watch and to hear. His own violin was a beautiful Spiritus Sorsana. He occasionally would have instruments on loan from Hills to try, and I loved to hear him play my own violin, for he made it sound wonderful.

I remember purchasing a fine Vuillaume bow from Beare's for eighteen guineas (a lot of money in those days) and Mr Lasserson proudly showed it to Max Jaffa, who followed me for a lesson. Max, in turn, proudly showed me his newly acquired Petrus Guarnerius violin. I remember, also, Mr Lasserson showing me the picture of himself in Leopold Auer's class in St Petersburg, together with many other famous violinists, including Heifetz – whom he beat in a competition. He told me once of a wealthy lady pupil who "surely must play Bartok. I adore his music." Mr Lasserson replied, "My dear, you must first learn to play Mozart!"

His extraordinarily sensitive ear led him continually to correct his pupils' playing for discrepancies of intonation, and he would always advise his special fingerings, which he would pencil in rapidly. I tried once, after listening to some recordings, to copy

Heifetz's style, and Mr Lasserson commented, "No! That's all right for Heifetz, but not for you!"

Mr Lasserson was always kind, and patient, and altogether a most lovable man. He was very conservative in his tastes, both in dress and in music. I will always remember him with great respect and admiration, and gratitude for raising my musical standards.

Harold Colman is one of a family of violinists, first taught by his father and his brother. He studied with Sascha Lasserson from 1947-1950, while playing in the New Theatre Orchestra in Northampton. He taught and freelanced, played in the Midlands Chamber Orchestra, and Northampton Symphony Orchestra. He has conducted youth orchestras, and presently conducts the Kettering Symphony Orchestra.

Robert Colman
by Gweneth Colman

Robert was largely self-taught as a child, and was considered to be a prodigy while growing up in Norfolk. Financial considerations loomed large, to an extent that it was not until he was aged 20 that he was able to take advantage of proper teaching – first at the RAM, and then with Sascha Lasserson, with whom he studied for five years just before the second world war. He felt honoured to be one of Sascha's pupils and considered that he was quick to bond musically with his teacher. He often felt the strongly spiritual nature of Sascha's interpretations.

Sascha was, of course, a much older man, of great kindness and with a lovely soft voice. If he was enjoying making music with a pupil, the lesson would often go overtime – with Sascha smoking continually, as usual. Robert was in awe of him, a man of such huge standing in the profession, who had been one of the most distinguished pupils of Leopold Auer and contemporary with so many great players. He had the gift of seeing, at once, any fault or difficulty that a pupil might have, and correcting it equally quickly by both word and demonstration, always with encouragement, and his teaching had a lasting effect on Robert.

Horrific years of war service followed for Robert – in Greece, Crete, in Egypt. He took his violin everywhere, even making space for it in his tank – until he had to leave it on a beach in Greece while he escaped by swimming out to a waiting destroyer; he hoped that it might be rescued by a musical German before it could be damaged.

On his return to Cairo he played on Cairo Radio with the Symphony Orchestra, with the strings of the Area Military Band and with ENSA groups supporting various visiting artists. He also founded and led the English String Quartet. Back in London, Robert was at once appointed to Sadler's Wells as soon as the orchestra leader heard that he had been a pupil of Sascha. He played for the International Ballet and then joined the Bournemouth Symphony Orchestras, to become one of its longest serving members, occasionally leading it, as well as playing a lot of chamber music and teaching in addition.

His star pupil, Anthony Flint, is well-known in Europe as concertmaster and soloist, and likes to speak of Robert as his teacher. Henceforth we will urge him to add that Robert was himself a pupil of Sascha Lasserson, so that the present generation will remember that great teacher and the tradition he embodied.

Robert Colman was virtually self-taught as a violinist until going to Sascha Lasserson, with whom he studied for five years. He was in the Bournemouth Symphony Orchestra for thirty-seven years and also played in the Wessex String Quartet.

Pauline Craft

Sascha Lasserson completely changed my life and I will be forever grateful to him. Hardly a day passes when I don't think of him and hear the words 'You will do better.'

His magic is hard to define because everything was so straight-forward and simple. When practising, just having his picture in the room makes me stop and think. I truly loved him for his kindness and absolute honesty. He never passed any mistake and always said exactly what was wrong and immediately demonstrated, with the violin a few inches away so that one could see those marvellous fingers at work. Sascha had an absolute genius for choosing just the right music to sort out the current problem, making the geography of the violin absolutely clear. If he ever said 'good,' I walked on cloud nine for a week, because he only said that on very rare occasions.

I have several wonderful memories I would like to share. The first was his own playing. I had taken Geoffrey Pratley to a lesson to accompany me in the Beethoven *Spring Sonata*. Sascha thoroughly approved and was nodding away behind Geoffrey, making signs to show how good he thought he was. The lesson went on with no thought of time and Sascha demonstrated whenever necessary. As I was packing up, Sascha was talking to Geoffrey and asked him if he knew the Glazunov Concerto, which he did (from memory). Sascha was thrilled and proceeded to play the whole of the first movement with him. I was lucky enough to be treated to a never-to-be-forgotten performance by the two of them.

Sascha's total lack of pretension was amply demonstrated when I saw him at a recital given by Mischa Elman at the Festival Hall. He was on his own and so was I, so he asked me if I would like to meet Elman. As we went round after the recital, he was worrying about a note that he thought was wrong in the Handel Sonata and was determined to sort it out with Elman. We joined the queue waiting for autographs, and I will never forget Elman's face when he saw Sascha; an ecstatic torrent of Russian poured forth as he threw his arms round him. Sascha had said I should meet Elman, so he broke off and introduced me. Elman just managed to smile and shake my hand, but all the time was saying, "You'll stay to tea, you must wait." The last I saw was Sascha sitting happily in the corner by Elman's case, while Elman despatched the queue at top speed.

Sascha didn't like exams very much, but one day he saw I was depressed and asked what was wrong, so I told him I was struggling with an aural exam. So, to cheer me up, he said, "Don't worry, Prokofiev couldn't do aural." I just loved that and always tell my pupils; it never fails to lift the spirits.

My favourite story is not my own; it was told to me by a then member of the LSO. On one of Heifetz's last visits to England he was rehearsing for a recording and had invited Sascha to be there. Sascha came in and sat quietly down to listen, but after about five minutes Heifetz stopped and went over to him and said, "I'm sorry, Sascha. You'll have to go! You're making me nervous." I think that is just the greatest tribute of all. This quiet little man was in fact a giant both musically and personally, and I count myself very privileged to have known him.

Pauline Craft is a teacher and freelance violinist. She studied with Sascha Lasserson for eight years after leaving the Guildhall. She coaches the Croydon Youth Orchestra.

Geoffrey Creese

I think it must have been 1950 when I first heard of Sascha Lasserson. I was at Woolwich in my first year in the Royal Artillery Band. This was National Service plus, as I had (at that time) to join for five years as a regular in order to get into the Band (and of course the orchestra). I already played the violin on joining and then doubled on clarinet.

A very good violinist, Tony Robinson, joined us at Woolwich and advised me to take private lessons with his teacher – Sascha! So I duly went along to Ladbroke Grove and was accepted as a pupil. Because I was in the Army, Sascha very generously charged me half price – one guinea (£1.1s.)

Sascha was gentle and softly spoken. When illustrating a certain difficult passage from a concerto he would make it appear so easy – but he wasn't a showman! He smoked during lessons and frequently kept a cigarette in his mouth, even when playing. Ash sometimes fell onto his violin but luckily never seemed to do any damage!

I feel very privileged to have had the opportunity to take lessons with such a renowned and much loved teacher. Happy days!

Geoffrey Creese was a violinist in the Royal Artillery Band at Woolwich in 1950, during which time he had lessons with Sascha Lasserson. Later he was in the BBC Light Orchestra based in Bristol. Then he moved to the LSO, followed by the New Philharmonia for seven years – after which he returned to the LSO for twenty years, eventually becoming a freelance.

Benedict Cruft

When I was 13 I had been studying for five years with Rosemary Rapaport in the Junior Department of the Royal Academy of Music. When she sacked me over something that was not related to violin playing, my father, who had known Mr Lasserson since the thirties through Arnold Goldsborough, telephoned him to ask him if he would take me on as a regular pupil.

Some time in 1962 or early '63, I went along to the Tonic Sol Fa Institute in Bayswater to play to him and was accepted for weekly Saturday morning lessons, all of which, as far as I can remember, happened in an extraordinarily dilapidated back room of that almost completely moribund organisation. It crossed my mind at the time that there was little call for a system of notation that I had never previously encountered, and I would not be surprised if it was only his rental of a studio that kept them from bankruptcy. If I was the first pupil of the day in winter, and we arrived around the same time, there was a ritual that never ceased to alarm me. He would greet me warmly and ask after my family, if my father (who sometimes came along to play the piano) was not there, and turn on the gas fire. He would then take off his coat and get out the first of his innumerable Players Number 1 cigarettes, put it to his lips and light it, only afterwards throwing the burning match into the gas to ignite it with a tremendous bang. The cigarettes, of course, as I am sure everyone will remember, grew into a soggy, still smouldering pile in the ash trays, while the ash fell off the current one down the violin, something he never seemed to notice in the intensity of the lesson.

One of the first things about him to impress the new young pupil was his ability to go straight to the heart of a technical problem. For a few years various people had been trying to improve my tone production. I remember playing at a competition that was being adjudicated by Fred Grinke and his suggesting to me after-wards that my tone would increase if I put my third finger further over the stick. It made no difference as far as the 12-year-old could tell, but what did make a very obvious difference to the 13-year-old was being told that once you have travelled on a down-bow past the middle of the bow there is no more arm weight going through the string, so it is necessary to push down with your first finger against the thumb in order to create a spring to put pressure onto the string.

I was extremely lucky to be sent to him at an early age before my technical patterns had set too solidly, and to be moulded while young into a sensible posture. There was no dogmatic stating that something had to be done in a certain way, without a clear expla-nation of why this way would be more efficient, so in my case he never tried to get me to play without a shoulder pad, as he himself did, because he considered that my neck was probably too long.

Repertoire was approached in a systematic way to build tech-nique through a combination of studies, concertos and pieces. He himself seemed to have a huge repertoire of music that is proba-bly seldom taught nowadays, as well as the classics: Spohr and Vieuxtemps concerti as well as Mozart, Sibelius and Beethoven, Novacek and Franz Schubert's *L'Abeille*, as well as unaccompanied Bach. I remember him saying that you should not attempt Mozart until you could play Vieuxtemps and Wieniawski, as the simplic-ity was deceptive, and putting me through studies that were very much beyond my capabilities at the time, so that when I came back to them a few months later, I would find out how much I had improved. He was still, in his seventies, a superb violinist with a breathtaking virtuoso technique of a type that I could never have achieved. He used to play impossible pieces to me at the end of lessons, like Ernst's *Last rose of Summer* variations or Popper's *Papil-lons*, to give me a taste for real virtuosity and maybe, in a gentle way, to show me that there were many things that I still could not do.

He had a wonderful memory for music. Because of his bad eye-sight he used to have to take the music really close to his eyes if he wanted to check something, and I recall him saying that, when he was a boy, he had copied out every piece he learned, to fix it for ever in his mind's eye. Did he therefore rely on a photographic memory?

His patience and kindness were always present. I don't remember a single occasion when he was rude or irritable with me, and he nursed my fiddle-playing along until I was 17, making sure that I played enough in public, and getting my father to organise concerto performances with amateur and youth orchestras. I had left school (the Central Tutorial School for Young Musicians, that later became the Purcell School) when I was 15, to spend the majority of my time practising, and I worked hard under his kind and skilled guidance for a further two years. Unfortunately, this rather strange (and self-chosen) life for an adolescent, of staying at home, practising for most of the day and night, began to worry my thoughtful parents, who feared for my sanity if I failed to spend any time with contemporaries. I am afraid that their decision to send me to the Royal College in 1966 probably hurt him, though he was always friendly when we met at concerts afterwards, but I became even more grateful to him for the work he had done for me, when I realised at the RCM that I was about two years ahead of most of my contemporaries.

The link with the past still surprises me when I think about it. I have memories of him telling me first-hand stories of studying with Auer; of Elman and Zimbalist and himself as small boys timing each other to see who could play Franz Schubert's *L'Abeille* in the shortest time; of hearing the 8-year-old Heifetz being brought in to astonish the 20-year-olds; of his giving the first performance of Joseph Achron's *Hebrew Melody* in the Winter Gardens in St Petersburg, of his saying to me that of all Auer's pupils, the greatest musician and most moving performer among them was Joseph Achron but that Achron was so crippled by nerves that he never played well in front of more than ten people; and of a patriotic gesture that he and some colleagues made in 1905 to show their support for the country's war against Japan, that started as a group of them going out into the street to play patriotic songs and swelled into a vast crowd who were mistaken by the police for political agitators and charged by sabre-wielding Cossacks.

I think of him quite often, treasuring the memories of working with him. When teaching, his explanations of technical problems frequently come back – for me to pass on to another generation removed by a century from the time when he was, himself, a pupil.

Benedict Cruft studied with Sascha Lasserson for five years as a schoolboy before moving to the RCM. Subsequently he played in the LSO and Philharmonia before moving to Hong Kong in the 1980s. There he led the Philharmonic Orchestra and the Tononi quartet. Since then he has worked mainly in London recording studios. He has given frequent performances of Bach solo sonatas and partitas both in UK and Far East, and has recorded them for Tononi Records.

Angela Dale

Some of the happiest remembrances of wartime in Britain are the concerts given all over the country by organisations such as ENSA and CEMA (Council for the Encouragement of Music and the Arts, which later became the Arts Council). It was on a tour for CEMA that I first met Sascha and had the privilege of accompanying him in a number of concerts. We seemed to get on very well together from the very first meeting, and it was always a pleasure to make music with him.

His quiet, unassuming manner and of course his extremely elegant playing went down well with audiences both of troops and factory workers, who were often completely uninitiated in the art of listening to classical music! The one piece I particularly remember playing with him was *Melody* by Tchaikovsky, full of Russian pathos and charm, and a particular 'winner' in his groups of solos.

Those were hard-working days, when we would travel from place to place, doing three or four concerts from morning to evening, so we always had to make a quick getaway. This was when we younger players always had to look after Sascha. His marvellous musical memory did not really extend into ordinary everyday affairs; in fact he was quite absent-minded. It became a regular standing joke – "Make sure Sascha hasn't left his hat behind!"

In our few moments of relaxation I used to tell him about my 'new' husband, his difficulties in getting out of the Royal Marines and his urgent need to have some more good lessons to embark on his violinistic career. Sascha listened to my story with the greatest sympathy and interest, resulting in our eventually meeting with him and his wife at their flat in Ladbroke Grove. She always received us with warmth and kindness when Peter's lessons finally began. What a lovely start this was for us both, launching us into what has transpired to be a fruitful and enjoyable musical career together.

Angela Dale studied at the RAM with Victor Booth and Franz Osborn. She worked with CEMA during the war, when she met Sascha Lasserson and introduced her husband, Peter Mountain, to him. She was Professor at the Scottish Academy of Music and Drama and Orchestral pianist with the Royal Liverpool Philharmonic. She worked with Heddle Nash, Jean Pougnet, Henryk Szeryng (among others) and has given concerts and broadcasts in UK and abroad with her husband, as a duo ensemble (established in their student days).

Dennis East

I was a Japanese prisoner of war. I came home from four years' captivity and was approached by Boyd Neel, who asked me to return to his orchestra (I had joined it before the war) for an immediate tour. I told him I was in no condition to do so and he suggested that I should speak to Fred Grinke, the leader of the orchestra, who suggested I contact Sascha. Sascha gave me an immediate appointment for a lesson.

This lesson was a revelation. He was so calm and patient with me, coming as I did from working for nearly a year on that bloody Burma railway, crashing on foot through 136 miles of jungle into Burma. (This is a separate story, but seems relevant to show how I must have appeared to Sascha so soon after, in 1946.)

Sascha chain-smoked through all lessons with never any suggestion of impatience or frustration. The matter of, for example, intonation! The question of harmonic tuning as in chords, e.g. notes sounded together as opposed to melodic intonation. Even mixed modes, e.g. Mendelssohn Concerto 2nd subject, where the accompanying orchestra wind players must play in harmonic intonation whilst the solo violin must use melodic mode. This, and other matters, were a revelation to me.

As to repertoire: at my request (I seem to remember) I studied the Elgar violin concerto. I have been told that Sascha played this very concerto early on in his career. I found his fingering system somewhat 'old-fashioned', no doubt due to my pre-war teaching with Paul Beard, at that time the new leader of the BBC Orchestra. My recovery, violin-wise, with Sascha was very rapid: within a couple of years I memorised and played – with Norman Del Mar conducting – the solo parts of a number of modern concerti, including the Bartok concerto. I refer to these events in no sense of self-pride. I am much too old, in my 80s, to have any such coy thoughts!

It crosses my mind that it might be of interest to compare his approach to teaching with my earlier teachers. At 15, I was awarded an open scholarship to the RCM when I studied with Maurice Sons; he, in turn, had been with Wieniawski and later with Vieuxtemps. Sons was known as the smallest man with the biggest tone in the world – he was less than 5 feet!

Later, I was placed with Paul Beard, then the recently appointed leader of the BBC Symphony Orchestra. This was a totally new approach to teaching, which suited me but was not for everyone. Here was a broader concept of both fingering and bowing. A later teaching concept I experienced was that of Max Rostal, whom I consulted for a special reason and after Sascha's death.

These last four teachers were, in my opinion, all excellent in their own particular way, though not for each individual pupil. In my own case, Paul Beard was excellent for me coming, as he did, after the dry, somewhat pedantic teaching of Sons. It might be said of Sascha that he was too quiet and unexcitable: but in my view, after forty years of teaching my own students, his work stands out, and though I sometimes thought his bowing and fingering were worthy of 'modernising', I later concluded that he had never considered departing, even slightly, from his own teacher's (Auer's) strictures! After all, he did have the backing of his illustrious friend Heifetz, who disdained the use of 'fingered' octaves!

As to 'interpretation', I must confess that the demands of the BBC timetable (I was by this time a member of the Symphony Orchestra), exacerbated by my move out to Surrey and my appointment to Trinity College, meant that I had little time to continue lessons with Sascha.

I saw little of Sascha for long periods – but on one notable occasion, when I was in the orchestra to accompany Heifetz in a recording at Walthamstow Town Hall, Sascha greeted me with such warmth before he joined Heifetz. That was the word that summed up Sascha – warmth!

Dennis East went on a scholarship to the RCM at 15, to study with Maurice

Sons and later with Paul Beard. On his return from four years' captivity as a Japanese prisoner-of-war, he was offered a tour with Boyd Neel and was advised by Frederick Grinke to go to Sascha so as to rehabilitate his playing. Subsequently he joined the BBC Symphony Orchestra and was appointed to the staff of Trinity College.

Marta Eitler

I had a colleague in the London Philharmonic Orchestra, the late Kenneth Weston, who was a pupil of Professor Lasserson and who spoke so glowingly of him that I, too, wanted to have lessons with him. I was due to play the Brahms Concerto with the RPO at that time and so went to Professor Lasserson. He gave me very useful fingerings and also commented on various aspects of my interpretation. My lessons with him were occasional and more like discussions on the merits of an interpretation. He did not just criticise but would always discuss and demonstrate how to play the difficult passages.

He often told me about his time with Auer, and I remember him telling me that, when the political situation in Russia changed and certain State holidays were declared, he was the only one who turned up for his lesson as usual. Auer was very displeased that the others did not appear, for he believed that violin playing was the very essence of life and should go on regardless. Professor Lasserson was present when the young Heifetz arrived at Auer's class. Lessons were held collectively, with everyone present throughout the period, and everyone was astonished at Heifetz's playing. Afterwards Auer pointed to another student to play but, one after another, the whole class suddenly developed a headache or a sore finger, or felt unwell. At last, a Canadian student stood up and said, "I'll play." Auer retorted, "No you won't! You sit down!"

Professor Lasserson had a lovely sense of humour and, when asked if he liked the piano, he replied, "Oh no, the semitones are not close enough."

I have often though what an injustice it was that he was never invited to teach at the London music colleges, for so many would have learned so much. He was always so helpful and kind, and dedicated. My real regret was that I did not have a teacher like him when I was young. My early teachers were good, but none of them had such a good and warm heart with the ability to give such confidence and encouragement.

I often think and speak of him – always as Professor Lasserson. I have far too much respect to refer to him as Sascha. He loved his pupils, and cared for them. Equally, I loved him. I still miss him.

Marta Eitler is a soloist, teacher and orchestral leader. She was in the LPO in the sixties. She had lessons with Sascha Lasserson on an ad hoc basis – "When I needed advice I went to Professor Lasserson, for there was no finer teacher on the continent."

Rachel Godlee

I met Sascha Lasserson only once when my sister and I wanted some instruction while studying the Mozart Sinfonia Concertante. I liked his positive suggestions, so I mentioned that I had a problem with the string-crossing passage in the viola version of the Bach *Chaconne*; the demi-semi-quaver passage where the slurs cross the main beat of the groups of four. I played it to him, and immediately he said, "Be consciously aware of the specific movement of the lower arm." At once the difficulties were overcome. It was a good moment.

I was very impressed how he could pinpoint the problem so quickly.

Rachel Godlee, viola player, was formerly in the Hallé Orchestra for many years.

Miles Golding

I first got to know Sascha in mid-1974. David Bateman, a fellow violinist in the RPO where I was doing some extra work, suggested that I might be interested in approaching him for lessons. Subsequently I studied with him for the following three or four years. I was a 23-year-old, had arrived in England the previous year from New Zealand and was beginning to establish myself in the freelance life of London working with the RPO, BBC-SO, several of the smaller chamber orchestras, the Pizza Quartet, as well as a fair amount of chamber music. Whenever I found time to work on my own in this increasingly busy professional life I would phone Sascha, arrange a mutually convenient time with him and take the tube to Shepherd's Bush clutching my violin, some music, and the few guineas that he so unselfishly requested in return.

His style of teaching was deeply refreshing. In earlier years I had been fed a rather heavy diet of technically analytical 'methods' and had a few serious gaps in my technique. 'Schools' of violin teaching have been with us for decades, and there is a rich source of ideas from which a violinist can benefit in the many publications that are at his or her disposal from Leopold Mozart, through Spohr, Flesch and Galamian to the very fine recent work of Simon Fischer, to name but a few. However, a responsible teacher must not force a pupil into a technical mould; technique should develop from the pupil's own physiological, intellectual and spiritual resources. This was, for me, where Sascha excelled. Not once did he say, "That's wrong, do it like this." Not once did he put me down, or suggest that I wasn't up to something. If I was struggling with a particular bowing, for instance, he would suggest an exercise, a study, a different manner of looking at the weakness from another angle, which allowed my fingers, wrist, arm, to find their own solution. He wouldn't even necessarily make an observation that something was not functioning ideally; he'd just tell me to practise a particular study in a particular way. He taught me how to play scales, and how to enjoy playing them. We looked at concerti: Brahms (at last – I recall feeling mortified when, as an 11-year-old, I was not allowed to look at the Brahms because I was too immature) and, new to me, Spohr; we looked at studies – Dont, Rode, Kreutzer – and, for the first time in my life, they became alive and exciting. I began to feel that anything was possible. Milstein always warms up with Dont no.5, he once told me; I would come out of his cosy, smoke-filled studio feeling like Milstein himself, would look at the world going round Shepherd's Bush Green, and think to myself what a privilege to have spent the last hour-and-a-half with a rare and special human being. His extraordinary humility drew me to his knowledge, experience and heritage, and I look back now and feel that though we were in one way master and apprentice, in another sense we were equals.

In the summer of 1976, I played a recital in New Zealand House with a New Zealand pianist, John McAlpine, now living in Köln. Sascha helped prepare me for that: two Beethoven sonatas, Prokovief's 2nd, and the Douglas Lilburn sonata. I took the pieces to lessons, and we both played the programme to him. His support was invaluable. Of course, there was never any question that he would not attend the event, and to see his small, bent frame amongst the audience was thrilling. Afterwards, he came up to us, quietly and briefly expressed his pleasure, then left to take a taxi back home.

I sometimes work with children of 8 to 18, teaching, coaching and conducting. I've always felt that Sascha is still present, still teaching me, and I hope that I can pass on some of his warmth and humility to enrich another generation's lives.

Born in Australia, Miles Golding started musical training in New Zealand. He came to the UK, studying first with Eli Goren and then with Sascha Lasserson. He played with the RPO under Kempe, with the Meridian Chamber Ensemble and the Capricorn Ensemble. Has also played with the English Concert, English Bach Festival, and Collegium Musicum Ninety. Over the past twenty years, he has been increasingly involved with period music.

Richard Gordon-Smith

In 1973, having completed four years at the Royal College of Music, I was enrolled in a peripatetic teaching course in Streatham. The training college offered a choice of 'approved violin teachers', one of whom was a certain Mr Lasserson. As one of my colleagues highly recommended him, I made an appointment at his Sterne Street studio.

I confess to having had some misgivings when I saw the age of my new mentor – he was then already over eighty – but I introduced myself, and amused him by informing him that he was 'approved' by my college (of which he had never heard). He solemnly examined the form I offered him on which he was supposed to list the details of his career. He signed the blank form and returned it to me with the words, "I should tell them my life? If they don't know me, how come they approve me?" I was sure I had offended him in my naivety, but the twinkle in his eye soon assured me that I had merely been initiated into the wit of Lasserson, which was to become one of the chief joys of our lessons for the next five years.

As I soon discovered, his was a most individual personality, wholly wrapped up in the welfare and progress of his pupils. It did not matter to Sascha that other teachers, mostly of lesser reputation than his, were now charging a minimum lesson fee of ten pounds. His fee had been three guineas forty years ago, and it was three guineas now. As this was post-decimalisation, it meant £3.15p duly paid each time we met (he apologetically put this up to four guineas in his last couple of years).

Sascha asked what I wanted to do with my violin playing. He knew I was training as a teacher, but he sensed that I really needed to perform. I told him that I should like to be good enough to be a soloist or at least to play in an orchestra. "Well, you could be whatever you want," was his reply, "but in an orchestra you will not have enough time to practise."

Later he said, "So many teachers demoralise their pupils with unkindness, but I encourage everybody, all my pupils: I find out their good points to build on. This is the Auer method. Nobody likes to have their dirty linen washed in public!" He particularly associated this last phrase with technical matters. He would give any technical help that was necessary, but he saw the artist's real job as a journey of the soul through interpretation of the great composers' music. Technique was not to be studied for its own sake; it was a means to an end and something to be worked at behind closed doors.

Sascha always demonstrated anything he wished to impart. His own technique was both fluid and dazzling while, at the same time, seemingly effortless. "I never stopped practising," he said. He was chuckling one day as I went in and, when I inquired the reason, he told me that he had been practising that morning by the open window of an upstairs room. He had been playing a scale in very long, slow bows, senza vibrato; ("it must have sounded terrible!" he said) when the window-cleaner suddenly poked his head into the room. "How long have you been playing?" asked the man. "About seventy-five years!" Sascha mildly replied. The man snorted scathingly, "You should be better than that, then!"

Lasserson's pupils often had to play to each other (another essential element of Auer's method). I was learning the Heifetz arrangement of Dinicu's Hora Staccato. Sascha was in stitches the first time I played it to him – I had transcribed it from the 78 rpm record and, as the turntable rotated too fast, I had written the piece out in E major, a semitone too high! I, of course, went and bought the printed music the next day, and became rather proficient at up-bow and down-bow staccato. A few weeks later I arrived early and heard the end of another pupil's lesson. "Ah, Richard! Please show us your up-bow staccato! ... He is very good at this ... watch!" Sascha's violin was thrust under my chin. "Can't I take off my coat first, and warm my hands, please?" I protested, but the answer was, "What for? If you can play, you can always play, no excuses!" After my reluctant demonstration the other pupil politely expressed a wish that he could play the stroke as strongly as I. "You wish?" said Sascha. "Huh, I wish I could do it so well!" His psychology was immaculate, and without analysing the absurdity of the compliment, I gained six inches in stature and played with more confidence for the rest of the lesson.

Sascha was proud (who could not have been?) of his noble pedigree from Leopold Auer (he claimed to be Auer's longest-standing pupil, having studied with him for some fourteen years) and through Nicolai Galkin, back to Wieniawski. His pride in his abilities on the violin was an entirely objective phenomenon and not any kind of ego trip. It was part of the very special relationship, based on mutual respect, which he fostered with each pupil and between all his pupils. The demonstrations – his to us, us to him or us to each other – these were not 'showing off' but the anchoring of our theoretical knowledge and private practice in the security of a shared experience. "If you don't tell them how good you are, how will they ever know?"

This 'making the ego slave to the purpose' was demonstrated when an earnest reporter wished to interview Sascha for a magazine article. He pursued Sascha by phone calls and letters (one of which I saw), but when I enthused about the proposed exposure and asked how he had replied, he said, "Oh I did not write back! What do I need it for? Should I advertise for more pupils at my age? Maybe a few years ago I would have been glad of the publicity, but now ..?"

Sascha never owned one of the 'great name' violins, but his Spiritus Sorsana was a very fine instrument by any standard. He always mixed strings, a gut A with wound D and G strings – he said he felt that the arrangement suited the instrument better. A thin material pad lay between the violin and his shoulder, and the fingerboard was deeply grooved by his surprisingly long fingernails. As he was only about five foot in height, most of his pupils, myself included, had a convenient aerial view of any demonstrations – and incidentally of a large cigarette burn on the table of the instrument (of which he swore complete innocence). Sascha, who was a prodigious smoker, would hold a cigarette in his mouth while he was playing, and the pupil would anxiously hover with the ashtray as the ash slowly curled down towards the varnish!

The confident pragmatist would always win out over the moon-eyed optimist in Sascha's world. His was 'the art of the possible'. When I arrived one day with a fine violin, he played it briefly then said, "It works well! Can you afford it?" I confessed it would not be easy. He laughed and told me about a pupil who had recently brought him a Gagliano to try. "It was a very good violin, but she asked me if she should sell her house to buy it. I said – What! Are you crazy? So, you play on a fine instrument, but you have nowhere to live!" I gave the violin I was trying back to its owner the next day.

This great man, who played the Glazunov Concerto with the composer conducting, would happily give up his own time to support a student. A London vicar who knew my father asked me to give a recital in his church. Sascha helped me prepare a virtuoso programme, Wieniawski, Tartini, Bach, Kreisler and Delius, and insisted that I play the whole thing from memory ("because you can!" he explained). He then brought along a couple of his other pupils to help swell the audience numbers and treated the modest event as a major artistic triumph.

When Sascha became frailer in his last year, and travelling to his studio was no longer advisable, I was invited to his house for lessons. At the end of one such visit he said, "Jascha Heifetz is playing the Mendelssohn concerto on the radio in a few minutes. Shall we listen?" As we listened to the broadcast record and followed the score, Sascha virtually gave Heifetz a proxy lesson over the airwaves. He felt Heifetz played too fast and mechanically, and that the interpretation was somewhat shallow. Lasserson was probably one of the few people alive who had the right to make such criticism. The two went back a long way, to the early days of their lessons with Auer, when the ten-year-old Jascha in his little sailor suit sat in the front row of the twenty-year-old Sascha's recitals. Mileage like that confers privileges not accorded to us lesser mortals. "If I had such a technique," grumbled Sascha, "I would not be content to play like this!"

After thirty years, much of his advice still comes back to me:

"Play fast passagework more slowly; it will sound more brilliant if you can hear every note."

"To be a soloist you need four concertos – Mendelssohn, Bruch, Brahms and Beethoven; then you can travel!"

"When people whom you don't respect criticise you, don't listen – after all, what do they know?"

"Please remember, practise slowly!" (These were invariably Sascha's last words to me at the end of each lesson.)

When Sascha's wife died, he cancelled only one of my weekly lessons. In offering him my condolences the following week, I expressed surprise that he should work again so soon. I got that endearing Jewish shrug: "What, I should sit and cry all day? I have to work, there are people who need my help!" How right he was.

Even in his last year, after the tragic loss of his son, when Sascha was ill and in pain, the lessons continued. The top frequencies had been missing from his hearing for some time. We all knew this, so his demonstrations were no less valid. When one day, at the end of his second play-through of the Bach Chaconne (with barely a break between), he eased the violin off his aching shoulder with the words, "I am a little tired today!" I forbore to say that I wished I had the stamina to do in my twenties what he had just done in his eighties!

Well, time moves on – and nothing stays the same. Although I am becoming better known as a composer than a violinist these days, I still earn my principal living from the instrument as a member of the RLPO. From time to time I meet other Lasserson pupils, and we talk together of this gentle, noble genius who enriched our lives so profoundly. In violin playing, in music generally, and in life itself, Sascha Lasserson is as much an inspiration to me now as he was nearly thirty years ago.

Richard Gordon-Smith began studies at the RCM where, over a period of four years, his teachers included Antonio Brosa, John Ludlow, and Jaroslav Vanacek. After leaving the RCM in 1973, he studied with Sascha Lasserson for five years. He played in the Ulster Orchestra and then, in 1980, joined the RLPO, of which he is still a member. In addition to orchestral work, he has conducted many of his own works as well as those of other composers and is himself becoming better known as a composer than as a violinist.

Geoffrey Grey

After some four years of what might, euphemistically, be described as ill-advised tuition at the hands of one of the pillars of the establishment professors, I went to study with Sascha Lasserson. It was a near thing however, as my composition professor was trying to persuade me to go to Max Rostal at the time. Fortunately I couldn't afford his fees, and a friend of mine, Dr Maurice Lusty, an amateur violinist who collected violinists like most people collect postage stamps, told me unequivocally that Lasserson would be not only better but also affordable – and what's more I'd get a full hour's lesson.

My friend proved to be right, and within the first three months of study Lasserson had persuaded me to relinquish the grossly ugly Voigt shoulder rest which was turning me into an osteopath's nightmare, and to hold the instrument comfortably and efficiently. (This was something of an achievement as I had developed a strong conviction over the preceding four years that unless I had the violin firmly clamped between jaw and shoulder the wretched thing would go flying and I would have to leave the stage in shame, clutching my shattered instrument and amour propre to the sniggering guffaws of my peers.) The violin rested on the collar bone and was supported between the thumb and third knuckle of the first finger of the left hand. This works well if you are in a relaxed and upright position, and you don't have the weight of a shoulder rest to cope with. If it is held correctly, the weight of the head will keep it stable and its tendency to drop towards the right hand side of the body is checked by the left hand. When you shift to the higher positions the thumb follows the hand round and easily supports the instrument. One has to practise the changeover, of course, but that's what scales and arpeggios are for.

He also gave me simple and clear instructions on how the bowing arm really worked which were so comprehensive that I was able, for the first time, to play at the heel of the bow at any dynamic level with total confidence. This was a technique which had somehow eluded his more illustrious predecessor who had a problem with the lower half of the bow and had developed the pernicious habit of starting almost every phrase on an up-bow, a foible which, in later years, I noticed that a number of his pupils had not shaken off. Lasserson's teaching of the bowing arm was very straightforward. The arm was held at a comfortable level with the string one was playing on, and the elbow and wrist joints were thought of as being as near to right-angled hinges as possible. The bow-arm was divided into three main parts. From the tip to the centre was worked by the forearm; the middle to the heel by the upper arm; and the middle section was practised to ensure a smooth changeover from forearm to upper arm. He also gave some exercises for getting used to holding the bow which involved holding it vertically and working one's fingers and thumb along its length and back again, and also holding it horizontal without the support of the thumb. If you got it just right, you could even play, albeit lightly, quite efficiently.

Playing at the point and the heel, ppp, was another part of the training, and there was a nice little scale exercise in harmonics and double harmonics at the heel of the bow which helped to steady any pre-concert nerves. This balanced the hand and made sure that any incipient shakes were revealed and dealt with. A very good exercise for changing strings was to take a treble-stopping passage (Dont opus 35, No.1, for example), treat each chord like an Alberti bass and start on each of the three strings in turn, first with a down-bow and then with an up-bow. An extension of this was to start very slowly and on the same chord, increase the speed as much as sensible and then slow down. As Lasserson pointed out, getting fast was not so hard; the real mastery was achieved in slowing it down evenly and rhythmically. Variations in dynamics and different parts of the bow were also used. The only thing that puzzles me is why he didn't seem to favour going back to open-string practice for a lengthy period. It is, after all, quite a feature of the Russian school of training and presumably of Leopold Auer, with whom Lasserson studied. Perhaps he realised that sort of discipline would probably alienate students reared on the English School of Violin Playing, which is really a very amateurish affair. I find it encouraging that so many survive to perform as well as they do. However, it must be said that, in spite of the prodigious talent and musical ability native to this country, the shortcomings of basic technical groundwork are sometimes only too apparent.

With the left hand, Lasserson helped me get back the use of my fourth finger which had almost atrophied from lack of use! Another foible of my previous teacher was his reluctance to use this finger, as he had some odd notion that therein lay some inherent danger by its deployment. He had insisted on my using his own fingerings which of course did their level best to ignore the rogue and errant digit. This, of course, led to all sorts of imbalances not only in the left but in the right hand as well. The notion that one could actually shift on the fourth finger was, I think, as alien to him as the concept of a UFO landing in Marylebone High Street in the early 1950s. When I actually saw somebody shift position with perfect ease and control using the fourth finger, I realised I would have to broaden my horizons.

I don't remember Sascha Lasserson being all that enamoured of some 20th-century music, but for all that he was always a great help to me in any piece I brought to class. There was only one piece he refused to have anything to do with, and that was Monti's *Czardas*, which he said was rubbish, so he taught me *Zigeunerweisen* instead. He was never a tyrant about fingering or bowing as he knew perfectly well that everybody's hand is unique, and he would find a way to get the best results for his pupils. His teaching of the classics was always fresh and inspiring and his suggestions invariably sound and practical.

I had an added bonus being also a pianist, and on occasion would accompany some of his other pupils. He was a delightful man, and as far as I know, all his pupils held him in great regard and affection. It was said at the time that Ivry Gitlis, who allegedly went through violin teachers the way Imelda Marcos went through shoes, actually studied with him for three whole months! A record as far as anyone knew to the contrary. Lasserson used to charge something between £2 and £3 a lesson while, in the great wide world outside, prices were hiked up to match the size of some pretty gigantic egos. £15 or £20 was a lot of money in those days (I think I lived on about £4 a week), and that was often for only forty minutes and not always the most beneficial of tuition. I don't know whether things are much better today. I suspect not, and I do hear that teachers are still handing out their parts for their students to copy in bowings and fingerings irrespective of their suitability. Lasserson was never lazy about this but would always help with such details at the lesson. He also gave advice on how to practise. Failing supervised practice periods, which certainly didn't happen in my day and, I believe, only happens at the Russian colleges and the Armed Forces Music Schools here, the best option is to make sure that pupils know how to get practical results in their practice periods, as opposed to mindlessly filling up the hours with repetition of their mistakes.

Lasserson was, of course, a very rare type of teacher, who genuinely cared for his pupils' welfare and paid attention to their needs, the only reward being the pleasure of imparting his knowledge successfully. I gained tremendously from the three years I spent with him, and am eternally grateful for his teaching and his genuine kindness to me. I probably use almost all his basic teaching in my playing, although there are quite a number of aspects I've developed for myself. One of his favourite exercise pieces was the *Moto Perpetuo* of Paganini, which can be played with so many different bowings and styles: it is a wonderful exercise for co-ordination, virtuosity and elegance. Lasserson also had quite a pawky sense of humour. Once we were talking about Menuhin, who even in those days, had developed a problem with his bowing arm; he had also embraced things Indian, including Ravi Shankar (whom he had introduced to the West) and, of course, Hatha Yoga. I was commiserating about Menuhin's problems, and Lasserson said dryly, "Well, what do you expect – standing on his head every morning?!"

Geoffrey Grey, violinist, composer and conductor, studied first with Frederick Grinke at the Academy and then with Sascha Lasserson from 1954 to 1957. He was principal second violin for the RPO and leader of the Bournemouth Sinfonietta. He is now Director of the Hermes Ensemble, which has performed many of his own works and other contemporary music.

Daphne Ibbott

Sascha Lasserson, the teacher spoken of with such affection by so many violinists over a number of years.

My own personal recollection of him is somewhat fleeting but nonetheless memorable. Nona Liddell and I were giving our first Wigmore Hall recital, and we went along to play through the programme to him. He spoke quietly, making pertinent small suggestions which I remember gratefully to this day. Nothing he said was in dogmatic vein, but rather as a discussion between equal musicians – an approach which means a great deal to youthful artists, when self-confidence and belief in one's own particular ideas are easily undermined.

Here, in Sascha Lasserson, we had not only a fine teacher, but a truly wise, gentle man.

Daphne Ibbott was a pianist, teacher and examiner. She gave many sonata recitals with Alfredo Campoli and Nona Liddell.

George Isserlis

Although not a professional violinist, I was anxious to improve my playing so as to get more joy out of music-making with my fellow amateurs. Therefore, in 1948, I joined Sascha as a 'mature' pupil and was to spend three fascinating years with him, during which he completely overhauled my style of playing.

Sascha was a delightful man, small in stature but big of heart. Although Russian by birth, he had forgotten much of his native language during the many years he had spent in the UK, without having completely mastered English. I tried to talk to him in Russian, which is my own native tongue, but soon reverted to English, which had become his more familiar language. Despite some linguistic difficulties he was an excellent communicator, but when occasionally he could not find an appropriate word to explain himself, he would take the violin and demonstrate what he meant.

He would instantly diagnose any faults in his pupils' style and gradually rectify them. In my own case he soon made me realise that the violin is a delicate instrument and must be treated gently. Under no circumstances must it be forced. As soon as I came to terms with this, my approach to the instrument became more respectful, forcing it ceased, scratches disappeared even when playing chords, bow changes became smoother, position changes became less audible, my intonation became more secure and the sound I managed to produce became more pleasant to the ear. All these changes he brought about without fuss and bother. They just happened. I loved my lessons and what little I know I owe to him.

My daughter, Rachel, started the violin at the age of 7 with a local teacher. Unfortunately the latter turned out to be unsatisfactory and, although we transferred her to excellent teachers, they could not loosen her up. When it became clear that she was not making any progress, I persuaded Sascha to take her on, and he worked a real miracle. In no time he got rid of her stiffness, and she then progressed by leaps and bounds. Today, she is a busy professional violinist.

Rachel Isserlis

I was lucky enough to learn with Sascha Lasserson from the age of thirteen for two years. There was a difference of over seventy years between us, but I was taller than him. He immediately put me on to difficult pieces such as the Kreisler-Pugnani *Praeludium and Allegro* and the Mendelssohn Concerto (in retrospect I can't imagine what they sounded like!) but I don't remember ever feeling under any sort of pressure during the lessons. I used to love watching his left hand in particular; his rather pale fingers looked so perfect on the fingerboard, as if they couldn't possibly be placed otherwise.

I am sure his wonderful way of demonstrating, playing on the pure gut strings with the greatest of ease whilst the ash from the inevitable drooping cigarette fell through the right-hand f-hole of his violin, has been described elsewhere in this book, as well as his reminiscences of the Auer days: for instance, playing *The Flight of the Bumble Bee* (or was it Paganini's *Moto Perpetuo*?) with a stopwatch, beating Zimbalist in this boyish contest.

Names were probably not his strong point; my friend Alison Bury, who also learnt from him during this period, was usually referred to as Berry Ellison!

I learnt a tremendous amount from Sascha during those formative two years and can never pass Shepherds Bush without thinking of him.

Rachel Isserlis was a pupil of Sascha Lasserson for two years before entering the RCM to study with Jaroslav Vanacek. Subsequently she studied with Herman Krebbers in Amsterdam. She now lives in Germany, and leads the Isserlis String Quartet.

Max Jaffa

Sascha Lasserson was a most loveable man, and a wonderful teacher of the violin.

In my case he became a lifesaver. I had had a few lessons from Sascha after I had left the Guildhall School of Music and Drama. But because of a heavy musical workload I hadn't seen Sascha for many years. On my demob when the war ended, I discovered to my horror – and after many abortive attempts – that I could not play the fiddle. I hadn't played for five years and eight months.

Feeling almost suicidal at the thought that I might never be able to play again, by chance Sascha and I came face to face in Oxford Street. He remembered me well, and we embraced. I, of course, could never have forgotten the great Sascha Lasserson. After the normal enquiries after each other's health, I asked him if he had time to have a cup of coffee because I wanted to talk to him seriously. It was indeed a heaven-sent opportunity for me to pour out my heart and tell him that I felt I could no longer play the violin. Sascha said, "Nonsense! Come to my house tomorrow and bring your violin." We arranged a time, and the next day – as almost by command – I took my violin to Sascha's house. He asked me to play. I told him I could not play, which he found difficult to understand. I well remember saying to him, "Sascha, I feel that possibly the only thing I can suggest – and if you are willing – would be for you to treat me as somebody who has come to you with a violin, and said, 'Mr Lasserson, I wish to learn how to play the violin. Will you teach me?'"

With his complete and immediate understanding of the situation, he agreed and we started at the beginning. He showed me how to hold the fiddle and the bow, and how to bring them together, as though I had never played before. He showed me how to practise and what to practise. For about six or seven months I went for a lesson four or five times a week, and played to him what I had practised. Earlier I have said that he became a lifesaver. He did save my life. To Sascha I owe it all.

To the end of his days, in my opinion, he remained – and will be remembered – for having been the greatest violin teacher this country has ever had the good fortune to possess.

Max Jaffa studied at the Guildhall with Max Mossel. Subsequently, when aged seventeen, he became leader of the Scottish Orchestra before returning to London to lead the orchestra at the Piccadilly Hotel as well as working in theatre, broadcasting, and films. Five years' war service as a pilot in the RAF left him unable to play until chance contact with Sascha Lasserson led to rehabilitation as a violinist, thanks to Sascha's help. He returned to free-lance work, with broacasting eventually leading to the Palm Court Orchestra, Grand Hotel – and ultimately Scarborough as Leader-Conductor of the Spa Orchestra for almost thirty summer seasons.

REPRINTED BY KIND PERMISSION OF 'THE STRAD'

David Jenkins

In 1973 I first went to Sascha Lasserson for lessons after recovering from a major accident which had put me in hospital the previous year. I had to learn how to play again, and nobody could have helped me more than Sascha. He gave me back my faith in the violin.

His lessons were held in an extraordinary studio, filled with antiques and works of art, and he would smoke continually through each lesson. He would often speak of my father, the violinist Tom Jenkins, who studied with him from 1950 to 1954, when Tom was at the height of his career as a broadcasting musician and people would speak of his dazzling playing. I remember Sascha telling me how pleased he had been to have him as a pupil, and I often heard how excited Tom was by his lessons, from which he would return each time with fresh insights into the music.

Sascha really gave me hope and belief again, both in myself and in my playing, and it was an inspiration to me to see how he coped with his own disability of severe arthritis affecting his hands.

David Jenkins began violin studies as a schoolboy with David Martin, before moving to the RCM to study with Hugh Bean. In 1972, following a major road accident, he was rehabilitated as a player by Sascha Lasserson, later taking up an award at the RCM to study with Carl Pini, himself a Lasserson pupil. Later still he studied with Yfrah Neaman at Guildhall, eventually moving away to work with the Orquesta Sinfonica in Las Palmas. Poor health caused him to leave the profession, but he remains a dedicated chamber musician.

Martyn Jones

I first went to play to Sascha Lasserson having been learning the violin for only 12 months. I found him most intimidating and, having heard my meagre efforts, he said that I was not of a sufficient standard to interest him. However, if I came back in a year he would listen to me again. I returned a year later and was delighted when he agreed to teach me. Sascha had already taught my father Tom and my brother Michael, and I felt proud to be following in their footsteps.

My first impressions of Sascha were of a dapper, old world figure, always in a dark three-piece suit, polished black shoes and with a cigarette permanently in his mouth. Mind you, his suit was always covered in cigarette ash and the lapels of his jacket badly crumpled. This was the result of not using a shoulder rest. It was his custom to turn the lapel of his jacket back and rest the violin on the inside; the jacket then gave a modicum of support and certainly stopped the violin becoming too flat. Mind you, it ruins your suits! Perhaps it is not coincidental that Mischa Elman and Nathan Milstein used to do the same thing.

He had a marvellous twinkle in his eyes and would demonstrate the most difficult passages with inches of ash hanging from his lips. I used to watch, fascinated to see if the ash would drop off and go into the f-holes of his beloved violin, a Spiritus Sorsana, I seem to remember. Very often it did, and now and again he would blow vigorously into the f-holes, and we both would start coughing in the ensuing cloud of ash. A non-musical point I remember about Sascha was the gas fire in the gloomy studios in Bayswater where he taught. In winter the studio was bitterly cold, and I always seemed to be the first pupil of the day. He would turn the gas on and then start a conversation and walk round the room tuning his violin; eventually he would strike a match and throw it at the fire. He did not have a good aim, and only after several attempts, with the inevitable explosion, would he succeed. Many was the time that I hastily moved several steps away from the fire, convinced that he had left it too long for comfort.

He was a marvellous teacher and it was invaluable for a young student to have such a technical grounding at an early stage. He was most insistent on scale practice but seldom listened to scales, leaving it up to you. He soon started me on some very difficult works; his thinking was that it was good to have attempted these pieces and having introduced the pupils to repertoire beyond their abilities, it would be highly beneficial when returning to the work at a later date. With this approach I ploughed through several of the Viotti and Spohr concertos as well as Vieuxtemps, Wieniawski and, later, the Khachaturian which, he insisted, was very good training for the ear. His memory was prodigious, and he could play anything requested. He often asked his pupils to play to the next person waiting for a lesson; this I always found embarrassing, as I knew very well that they were all much better than I was. But in Russia he had learned in the class system of Leopold Auer, and he felt this passed on some of the benefits of the class lesson system, which at that time was simply not in vogue in the UK.

I studied with Sascha for three years before going to the RCM. It was a very sad day when I said goodbye, as I knew that he always took the loss of a pupil very personally. However, once at the RCM, I moved into a flat in Ladbroke Grove, without realising that he lived in the same road, and often, on seeing him coming down the road, I would go out and say hello.

In the post-war years there was hardly a violinist in London that had not benefited from his teaching. It is disgraceful that he was never invited to teach at any of the colleges of music. This robbed the country of the unique opportunity of having a direct line of teaching from the world-famous Auer school.

Some years later, when I was playing in the LPO, we were privileged to perform with David Oistrakh on his last appearance in London. At the rehearsal I saw Sascha come into the auditorium of the Albert Hall, and at the break I went to chat to him. Sascha always went to see the older generation of Russian violinists when they were in London, but he said that Oistrakh would not know him, and it would be embarrassing. However, I persuaded him to come back stage and took him into the green room. Oistrakh immediately recognised him from photos he had seen of the Auer master class, and gave him a great bear-hug. They chatted away in Russian for some ten minutes or so. Sascha was very moved by this meeting, and was more than dewy-eyed when we left.

Martyn Jones studied with Sascha Lasserson for three years before going to the RCM. Subsequently he joined the LPO, and later played under Klemperer in the Philharmonia, whose Archivist he eventually became.

Michael Jones

Sascha Lasserson was the great exponent in England of the celebrated Auer school of violin playing before and after the second world war. He told me that he was touring the country just before the first world war as a soloist, with a Russian ballerina, and when the war broke out he decided to remain here, to the benefit of so many British fiddlers.

My father, who was a very well-known player, broadcasting regularly from the Grand Hotel, Eastbourne, in the early thirties and making many records at that time, would hear of me going to no one other than Mr Lasserson for lessons, which started towards the end of World War II, when I was about 14, and continued for several years.

I arrived for lessons knowing that virtually every well-known fiddler in London had been through Sascha's hands at one time or another, and consequently I felt nervous. This feeling was quickly dispelled by the humanity and warmth of Sascha's personality and his genuine interest in each of his pupils. The real cause of one's nervousness was one's own inadequacy.

There was a large photo on the piano in the room where he taught in St Quintin Avenue. This was of Leopold Auer together with his class in St Petersburg, and Sascha, as a boy of 11, sitting cross-legged on the floor in front of the adults.

Sascha's teaching consisted of a thorough grounding in the studies and repertoire of the 19th century, all of which he could play beautifully and impeccably at the drop of a hat. He had a repertoire of over fifty concertos, but paramount was the playing of unaccompanied Bach. Auer apparently was of the opinion that if you could play the sonatas and partitas you could play anything. It was, of course, before the days of 'authenticity' and the quasi-academic approach so prevalent now, and Lasserson's playing of these works was basically melodic, with a warm, cultivated sound but with due regard for the structure and shape of the music. A great treat at lessons was when he played a movement to you, especially the *Chaconne*.

He had the great ability to encourage players and often to improve them out of all recognition. This was aided by the charm and sympathy of Mrs Lasserson, who used to preside at his occasional musical evenings for pupils, when 'party pieces' were performed.

Among those lucky enough to have studied with him and known him, he is an abiding memory.

Michael Jones was a member of the Boyd Neel, Jaques, and Philharmonia Orchestras before going on to lead the Northern Sinfonia. He was a member of the Amici Quartet and later became a freelance player in London

Homi Kanga

After I obtained my Premier Prix from the Conservatoire Nationale de Paris, I was advised by my friend Tom Jenkins – who was a pupil of Carl Flesch – to take a few lessons with Sascha Lasserson.

I went to Sascha for a few months before I joined the LPO and obtained from him many fresh ideas regarding bowing technique and fingering.

He was a kind and sympathetic man, and I always enjoyed my lessons with him.

Homi Kanga was a long-time member of the LPO, whose membership of which was preceded by a period of study with Sascha Lasserson – as recommended by another Lasserson pupil, Tom Jenkins.

Mary Kennard

I first went to Sascha Lasserson in 1965, when I was about 40. He always referred to me as 'the young lady' – very flattering! I had trained at the Royal Academy during the war, with Rowsby Woof and later, for a short time before my daughter was born, with Albert Sammons. Because of the war, and Woof's death, and my going abroad later, my career was very disjointed, and I did not take up the violin seriously again until the early '60s. I was shocked to find how badly I was playing and went to see Philip Hill, an old friend from student days, for advice. He said at once, "You must go to Sascha Lasserson." I asked if he'd take me, and Philip just smiled and said, "Go!"

My first impression of this great little man was of his wisdom, warmth, and gentleness. When he played, it was magic. He asked me to play a bit of the Bruch G Minor slow movement, and after a few bars he stopped me, saying, "You can make a violin sing. I will take you. You couldn't play the last movement of the Mendelssohn Concerto, could you?" I said, ruefully, "No." He replied, "Don't worry. You will!"

I studied with him almost until his death, and he taught me so much. The first piece I had to prepare was the Bach C Minor unaccompanied sonata, very difficult for me then and horribly revealing. His understanding of Bach was profound and his teaching of Bach superb, with so much colour and interest. He used to say that people treated Bach with too much awe, but – after all – Bach was human and did have sixteen children! He told me that Auer, at the competition for the Gold Medal at St Petersburg, would shut his eyes and stick a pin in one of the Bach unaccompanied sonatas. Whichever one it was had to be played by the candidate – and all candidates were expected to be able to play all the Bach unaccompanied works from memory.

Sascha would often play to me. He had an amazing arrangement of *The Last Rose of Summer* – so difficult as to be almost impossible for anyone except himself and Heifetz. I remember him telling me about Elman, who never took any music with him on his travels. He once played to Sascha the Bach C Minor Sonata and Sascha queried one chord that Elman played. They had to search London to find a copy of the work, which proved Sascha to be right.

He knew Glazunov and had given one of the first performances of the concerto with the composer conducting. He loved Albert Sammons and I believe that, if one of them was away, each would help out with the other's pupils. Sascha felt that Sammons was really underrated in this country, and that he played the Elgar Concerto much better than Kreisler – although Kreisler was its dedicatee.

I had a 1618 Amati at one time; Sascha loved it and would grab it and play to me. I came in one day to find him most upset. He had forgotten that he had put his violin on a chair and had sat down on it. Hill's had to put it together again, and he said the shock nearly killed him.

Sascha hated music to be rushed, and once told me of an American pupil who played the last movement of Mendelssohn Concerto so fast that Sascha could not bear it. He said to me with a twinkle, "I told him to play it slower, and he couldn't do it! No control!" Sascha would make his pupils play Paganini Caprices at different speeds to gain that control.

I started to play for the Council for Music in Hospitals and he helped me so much, taking the same trouble over a minor work as he would with a great one. He taught me to play with total commitment to any audience and told me how he had once played for an audience of charladies. I remember learning Achron's *Hebrew Melody* with him. He had given its first performance in Russia and he wove a story round it for me, telling me to imagine it when I played. I always tell an audience about it when I play it now.

I loved to hear him talk about the old days in St Petersburg with Auer and Elman and Heifetz – all men of genius. Sascha was their equal, but with an added genius, that of the great teacher. He had the amazing gift of making one relax. I would watch him, and try to copy him, and find myself playing things I would not have dreamt I could ever play. He would give wonderful fingerings to make difficult passages possible, but he was never dogmatic about it. He would say, "Now, in this passage you can do this way – or that way," and let you find out which was best for you.

He would often say, "I wish you had come to me earlier," and I would reply, "Yes, I might have had a decent technique." He would reply, "In England you talk of technique as if it is solely facility, but in Russia it is everything – tone, musicality, etc so do not say you have no technique."

I owe him so much. It was a privilege to have studied with him, but how I wish I had come to him sooner.

Mary Kennard studied with Rowsby Woof at the RAM and also for brief periods with Max Rostal and Albert Sammons. Wartime and family commitments prevented a professional career. Much later she was advised by Philip Hill to go to Sascha Lasserson, and studied with him for twelve years. She has taught in schools and further education colleges; has given several recitals with Daphne Ibbott, and has been involved for many years with the Council for Music in Hospitals.

David Lasserson

The jazz violinist Johnny Van Derrick enjoyed a long and colourful career as a performer and recording artist. His sound is better-known than his name, since he was the violin soloist for Henry Mancini, a role he filled for twelve years, covering many of the most celebrated film scores, including The Pink Panther. Johnny's sweet and distinctive playing was also recognised by advertisers, who used it to sell everything from insurance to train tickets. After his death in 1995, it was a curious sensation indeed to hear him still playing on a Renault Clio television commercial. His two CDs in his own name, *Always on the Fiddle* and *Gershwinning*, demonstrate his unique combination of a virtuoso technique and a devilish swing.

Johnny studied with Sascha for six years and openly acknowledged his debt for the remaining thirty years of his life to anyone who would listen. When we first met in a wine bar in Soho, where he had been playing his heart out with guitarist Denny Wright, I confessed to him that I was teaching myself jazz fiddle. He launched into a potted autobiography, in his cheeky cockney voice: "I went to Brussels Conservatoire at the age of 12, won a silver medal ... there can't be too many of them around ... then the Jerries came in, and that was the end of my classical studies. I took up the trumpet during the war, then came back to the fiddle, and studied for six years with a chap called Lasserson." I don't know who was more surprised by the coincidence – in jazz circles Johnny wouldn't have met anyone who knew about his beloved teacher, and here was another Lasserson asking him for lessons.

I started going to Van Derrick's house in Denham and was surprised to find that he taught me no jazz whatsoever. The frail-looking man, who had had heart disease for twenty years, took me through a three-hour assault course of exercises and drills, with a major emphasis on Sevcik, Mendelssohn and the virtuoso classical repertoire. "We'll soon have you going up and down the fiddle," he said. Of the many references he made to Sascha, it was vibrato that he kept coming back to. He insisted on a vibrato with life centred in the finger and not the upper arm, so as to keep intonation intact. "Listen for the note inside the note." When we played together at his regular Sunday night gig in Wandsworth (for which he was paid embarrassingly little), he leaned over and said, "Watch your vibrato, Dave. It's a bit oy-oy-oy. Your uncle would never have stood for it."

I found in Van Derrick a spirit that united several worlds that, until then, had seemed to be disparate. He was a link to my family history, since Sascha died before I could benefit from lessons with him. He combined classical music with swing, quoting the concerto repertoire in his jazz solos. He was theatrical, entertaining his audiences visually by pretending to make left hand pizzicato notes come from the top of his bald head. He spoke Yiddish, which he learnt from his émigré colleagues while playing in commercial string sections. He made violins; he never lost his love of trumpet playing; he was politically active in the Musicians Union; he followed acutely the twists and turns of government arts policy,and championed the rights of the working man. He had been an orchestral player, but was dispirited by the working conditions. This was a man who could not rest.

There was also an emotional depth behind his serenading, which came from the fragility of his health, and from his disturbing war experiences as a youth on the convoys to Russia, an episode which haunted him. His influence is considerable, and unsung – much like Sascha's. It is unlikely that any British jazz string players exist who did not at some time benefit from Van Derrick's help, and listen to him talk about Sascha Lasserson. The final straw would always be the end of a lesson, when he would blush at the question of payment, and suggest five pounds. This brought on a further homage to Lasserson and his generosity to a generation of British violinists: "He was kind to us, and that's rare." It also brings out a fundamental similarity between the two men, and perhaps a trait that Sascha's gentle example engendered. The delicate art of fine string playing draws from its practitioners a lifetime of loving dedication.

David Lasserson studied jazz violin with Johnny Van Derrick, himself a pupil of Sascha Lasserson. After reading English at Oxford, he entered the RAM as a postgraduate student to study viola with John White. Later he studied with Bruno Giuranna in Cremona. He has been freelance since then.

Malcolm Latchem

In the years following my studies at the Royal College of Music, and while enjoying my first professional work, I was encouraged to approach Sascha Lasserson for lessons.

Although I had perhaps only twelve or so lessons, they were memorable – memorable because, throughout my working life all the points Sascha made have remained with me, both in performance and while teaching. I am sure many will write about Sascha's bowing system, which afforded me a wonderful insight into the Russian school of violin-playing.

My bow arm was dreadful! I had far too high an elbow position, and I used the upper arm far too much. My lasting memory of Sascha – who, in height, just reached my shoulder – is of him grabbing my upper arm as if in a vice and forcing me to use just my forearm. Unfortunately, physical contact is frowned upon these days, but how often would I have liked to have seized the upper arm of a frustrating pupil!

Sascha had much to offer every player. Teachers and their students would go to him – sometimes to their mutual surprise and embarrassment, as they came face to face before or after a lesson!

Malcolm Latchem studied with Albert Sammons at the RCM before going to Sascha Lasserson; at that time he began an orchestral career in the RPO under Beecham. He led his own string quartet in New Zealand and broadcast as a concerto soloist. Returning to the UK as a founder-member of Academy of St Martin-in-the-Fields, he combined this with five years in the Philharmonia. Subsequently he was sub-leader of the LPO. A member of the Dartington String Quartet, he taught violin at Dartington College of Art and the Universities of Bristol and Exeter. He was a player-manager of the ASM's Chamber Ensemble from 1972 to 2002 and was awarded an honorary degree of Master of Music in 1980 by the University of Bristol.

Harry Legge

After spending the last two years of the war in Nigeria (not the place to play much music!), I arrived in London, and on the way home to Northants where my family was then living, I rang a friend in the business and found myself at Denham Studios the next morning – still in tropical kit and a bush hat! Apart from causing a stir by my outfit, it was clear that my playing did not meet with universal approval as I was hopelessly out of practice. The advice from my colleagues was unanimous – "Go to Lasserson." Unlike many of my friends, I had not been to him before the war, but it did not matter; he took me on and I had several lessons (paying in cash as I went). In those lessons I learnt the whole essence of string playing which, in all my lessons at music college, I had never appreciated. I have based my technique on what I learned from Sascha, and anything that I have done since has been based on those crystal clear principles he enunciated.

Many violinists and viola players have based their playing on his teaching – many of them going to him 'on the side' whilst they were officially learning at one of the colleges. One of the best examples is Max Jaffa who found he could not play at all after the war where he spent his time flying aeroplanes, and had to start again from scratch with Sascha (whom he had luckily bumped into in the street), and within a few months was playing better than ever. Sascha said he was perhaps the best talent he had ever come across, "but perhaps a little lazy!"

My son Anthony is now Head of Opera at the Royal Academy. As a student he studied the violin as a very second study. I persuaded Sascha to give him a few lessons so that when he found himself dealing with professional violinists in the course of his work he, although not a violinist, would know the principles involved, and who can really play and who cannot.

Harry Legge was a long time member of the RPO under Beecham. He studied with Sascha Lasserson on returning from war service in Nigeria. He founded the Edinburgh Rehearsal Orchestra and trained and conducted the Brent Symphony Orchestra for many years.

Robert Lewin

Only a few weeks ago a young violinist was enduring the ordeal of an audition with one of the London orchestras. Asked about study qualifications and the like, the reply was, "I am with Lasserson." For the next few minutes auditioning was shelved as everybody present who had ever held a violin under his chin eagerly gathered round – "Ah, dear old Sascha – so he's still teaching – how is he?"

And now Sascha Lasserson has gone. He died on July 6 at the age of eighty-eight. His lifetime was truly devoted to the violin, and as a teacher he had no peer.

To write an account of somebody who has had a tremendously long and busy life is likely to be a prodigious task. With Sascha Lasserson the summary is soon told. He was born in Russia in 1890; his father was a professional violinist who gave him his first lessons; at the age of ten he studied with Nicolai Galkin (a pupil of Wieniawski and Vieuxtemps) but, soon after, came under Leopold Auer at the St Petersburg Conservatoire, staying with him for 14 years, during the latter part of which he became a student teacher. Many of the most famous violinists in the world would have been coached by Lasserson, with his first teaching experiences coming so early. He made some notable solo appearances, playing the Glazunov Concerto with the composer conducting. In 1909 he received the Gold Medal Diploma of the Conservatoire, capped some two years later by the Highest Distinction Award, the top academic prize a violinist can achieve. Meanwhile his press notices proclaimed him as having an astonishing mastery of the violin coupled with a remarkable musical sensitivity.

In 1914, at the age of twenty-four, he came to this country where he gave recitals, played concertos and was much praised for his series of broadcasts that included the complete ten Beethoven sonatas. Digressing for a moment, I was once 'sitting in' at Lasserson's studio in Shepherd's Bush when a pupil came in bringing with him an ancient newspaper. It was dated November 12 1918 and the reason for its long survival was of course that it contained the account of Armistice Day, but there on the front page were the concert notices, and in a prominent place a certain Sascha Lasserson was to play the Elgar Concerto at the Queen's Hall.

He had already begun to take pupils and, as his reputation grew, so his studio in London became a magnet for violinists from all over the world – they even came from Russia, that traditional home of violin learning. He married, and some three years ago his wife died, also one of his two sons. About a year ago the doctor gently suggested he might give up the studio – after all, the students could just as easily come to his home. He was teaching almost to the end.

That is Sascha Lasserson's life story. He was a modest, unassuming person who never became a household name. Once, in an article, I said that you have to be a violinist to know the name of Lasserson, but there can be few players this century who do not know it.

For all his remarkable gifts as a teacher I do not believe it was his first choice of vocation. As a violinist Lasserson belongs to the very top rank of players, but that is not quite the same thing as being a born soloist. Violinists nowhere near his standard have made the grade and become popular stars – Lasserson was not of that breed. To project yourself so that the public is irresistibly drawn to you in vast numbers is one of those personality enigmas impossible to evaluate. People who think that everything in life is ordained and nothing ever happens by chance might see in Lasserson an example of how a concatenation of events has proved an immeasurable boon to us. It is our good fortune that Lasserson's comparative failure to attain instant stardom turned him towards teaching. If he did not captivate the concert hall crowds the intimacy of the studio was the place where his musical presence came to life; part of the secret of Lasserson was the influence he exercised, the inspiration that made you play better, a gift much rarer than the concert performer who dominates his public.

Violin technical skills have never altered in essence. In the privacy of the studio you learn by example, that human propensity to copy, even mime, the person you admire. Besides setting a marvellous standard to follow Lasserson had the remarkable faculty of analysing your faults, their underlying cause with an instinctive feel for the cure. Nobody who went to him will fail to recall the astounding speed of his reactions. That mind of his worked like lightning and the words – in that never to be forgotten Russiantinged accent – came tumbling out. Good players and bad, we all have our technical hurdles and weaknesses that we try hard to conceal, but they were an open book to him. To Lasserson they were a challenge to his powers to overcome them. If you tried hard enough he was by your side to help you to win. As the demand for his services grew, he never succumbed to the temptation to be selective. Other great teachers are disposed to pick the sort of material that will develop fastest and do them most credit. Lasserson's pride was to take the least promising and make something of them too. Somehow or other he would fit you into the schedule. Did he ever refuse anybody? Well, I can think of one case, the mother who directed him to teach her daughter all the standard concertos. Lasserson mentioned scales and kindred preliminary matters, but mother was adamant. Concertos only! Suddenly Lasserson realised he was so full up he was unable to oblige.

It was only in the later years that he would take a little time off and he liked to talk about violinists. His fabulous memory could recall listening to Sarasate in Russia. He knew all the great ones, he could praise them, also he knew their shortcomings. Some of the dazzling virtuosos are slaves of their own impetuosity, and then he would pick up his violin, the Spiritus Sorsana to which he was faithful all through the years, to demonstrate the argument. First he rattled off the Paganini Caprice No.24 at lightning speed and then he played it again at a true allegro moderato, showing what an alluring piece of violin music it is when taken like this, with perfect rhythm and disciplined control.

He never ever gave a piece of violin advice that was not practical, down to earth and simple to follow. Yet the man who could be so clear sighted when it was anything to do with the violin could sometimes seem a little old-fashioned in his late 80s. I was to take him to Hill's at Missenden – he had not seen their new place – and of course his violin wanted servicing; those ever strong fingers of his took no time at all to dig holes in the fingerboard. It turned out to be one of those burning hot days in that ferocious summer of 1976 with the temperature was well into the nineties, and as I drove up punctually at 9.30 in shirt sleeves so at that precise moment the front door opened and out he came, perfectly attired in formal black coat and striped trousers and over all a most beautifully cut and well preserved overcoat from a former era; the hat at just the correct angle, and he was bearing his violin case together with a neatly furled umbrella. "Sascha," I said, "Please, please – you won't want the umbrella."

He loved to hear from his pupils and their success meant a lot to him. Their letters from all over the world were carefully preserved, like the one from Elisabeth Matesky telling of her recital at the White House with President Jimmy Carter an intent listener. It never occurred to him that any out of that legion of violinists owed him anything. Old men forget, but then he never grew old. I am sure that all those who went to him will treasure their remembrance of the diminutive figure who was so wonderful a player and teacher, but even more a loveable person. An endless array of violinists of every degree of talent passed through his hands; they were proud to be his pupils. Nobody ever had so many, but not one of them while they live will ever forget Sascha Lasserson.

Robert Lewin was a freelance violinist, who had some lessons with Sascha Lasserson and went on to become - in addition - a dealer in stringed instruments. He was a frequent contributor to The Strad, writing on many aspects of violin playing.

REPRINTED BY KIND PERMISSION OF 'THE STRAD'

Nona Liddell

Though I had lessons from Sascha for only eighteen months, more than forty-five years ago, his influence on me was very lasting and I have never ceased to be thankful that I had contact with such a great teacher and special human being.

When I was a pupil I used to go to his flat in St Quintin Avenue, but much later he taught in a studio belonging to a great friend of mine, Bunty Lempfert. One day, when I was visiting her, Sascha completed his teaching and came out into the courtyard between the studio and the house, cigarette in mouth, preparing to leave. Having not seen him for some years, I was determined to catch him, dashed outside and we had a reunion, certainly joyful on my side. However, once a pupil always a pupil, and in hardly any time at all we were back in the studio, his violin unpacked and in my hands and I was being encouraged to demonstrate whether or not I could play the arpeggio at the start of the 5th Etude of Paganini (I couldn't)! Despite my failing this test, we stayed in touch and, to my enormous delight, he attended a concert in which I was performing at the Wigmore Hall, some months later on.

Nona Liddell's prom debut was at the young age of 20. She led the London Sinfonietta for twenty years and was awarded an MBE in 1992. Professor of Violin and Chamber Music, Trinity College, she studied with Sascha Lasserson in the 1940s.

Sir Neville Marriner CBE

I was an occasional pupil of Sascha – my motivation was to experience a different national characteristic in violin technique. My previous teachers – my father, W. H. Reed, George Stratton and Albert Sammons – gave me music aplenty without securing my technical ability to express it. Sascha had a unique intuition to identify physical problems, and a brilliant facility to demonstrate his solutions.

His approach to music was typically modest. He advocated rather than insisted, and you left his studio enjoying the freedom to express your own convictions with the added bonus of the possibility of a slightly more virtuoso facility.

Sir Neville Marriner, an occasional pupil of Sascha Lasserson, led the Marriner Quartet, and went on to found the Academy of St Martin-in-the-Fields. He was the Orchestra's first conductor.

Elisabeth Matesky

Sascha Lasserson was the embodiment of everything one imagines in a great musician and teacher. Although he was physically a small man, he had the aura, authority, and humanity one associates with the great figures of his time - and greatness needs no applause, often disdaining or running from it.

In 1963, I arrived in London on a Fulbright Scholarship for advanced violin study, following graduation from the University of Southern California. My first teacher was my father Ralph, who taught me all about beauty of sound. Following his Franco-Belgian approach, I moved to that of Leopold Auer by studying with Jascha Heifetz while at USC. I asked him with whom should I study in England if I received the Fulbright and, without hesitation, he replied; "Liz! Lasserson in London!"

On the Fulbright, one is assigned to a host University or Conservatory; mine was the Royal College of Music in London and, upon first acquaintance, I began my search for 'Lasserson in London'. Although I had the benefit of lessons with Antonio Brosa (who was a magnificent violinist, and a warm and compassionate man endowed with a colourful musical personality), I felt the 'pull' and need to find Mr Heifetz's revered colleague. It took eight months to learn his whereabouts from a classmate at the RCM, and by early May 1965 I was in Queensborough Terrace W2, waiting for the great man to greet me.

Lasserson's kindness and generosity with lesson time was astonishing; he gave three-hour lessons at one-hour prices, and seemed almost embarrassed to accept money. His complete mastery and memory of all the Spohr concertos as well as practically every other piece of violin repertoire was amazing for a man of 75. He played freely and movingly, and with the technique of a true master - and seemed happy with Mr Heifetz's referral of him as the teacher from whom to learn more technique and repertoire. As our lessons became regularised, he would tell me stories of his youth in St Petersburg – and there is so much to my relationship with Sascha that I will break it into sections

I

Lasserson's reaction to my violin schooling and performance at the beginning of May 1965 was most positive. He felt my sound was rich, but that it was "too much sound all the time". He felt my bow arm needed work and help for, at the initial meeting, I possessed a Franco-Belgian bowing approach with the use of the forearm and lots of wrist; my upper arm was not terribly involved in the process. Lasserson used the Preludio of the Bach E Major Partita to start to 'cure' my bow flaws. Levels of the elbow on the various strings were strongly addressed as we worked to get my whole right arm into one unit. Sascha taught me with enormous patience, and showed me how to practise the difficult bowing configuration.

He had me doing brush strokes and watching my arm levels while moving from the right shoulder in this passage, with a very strong kick on the fourth 16th note of each group of four 16th's. The point was to have a musically harmonic sense of direction in the conjoint motion passage which leads to the next section of this musical perpetuum mobile. Sascha instructed me to practise this "VERY SLOWLY, and to be patient." He was extraordinary at unravelling technical problems. He would sometimes put his hands on my left hand and, literally, move my fingers around so that I would physically feel what he wanted me to feel and then do. He gave me a group of left-hand exercises which I have used to this day, including the exercise for left-hand finger independence shown on the next page. This exercise should only be done for a maximum of five minutes at a time, and one must then relax the left arm quietly – as a dead weight.

Play 1234 on A String. Keep fingers down, then lift 1; move with bow to D String and repeat 1 – 0

Play 1234 on A String. Keep fingers down, then lift 2; move with bow to D String and repeat 2 – 0

Play 1234 on A String. Keep fingers down, then lift 3; move with bow to D String and repeat 3 – 0

Play 1234 on A String. Keep fingers down, then lift 4; move with bow to D String and repeat 4 – 0

This exercise should only be done for a maximum of 5 minutes at a time, and one must then relax the left arm quietly – as a dead weight.

2

As my bow-arm began to take on – for want of better words – a 'Russian' bow-grip, my left hand began to become more supple in double-stopping and also in the higher positions, because Lasserson insisted on playing on a slant to let the fingers literally cave in at the last joint and become more like pads as one navigated into the higher positions. He assigned me more repertoire, including his beloved Glazunov concerto, to highlight the technical virtues he was adding to my playing. We spent well over a year on the Glazunov and, during that period of intense study, my intonation and bowing ripened into a purity I had not previously known. Once again, Lasserson emphasised practising all the various tricky passages slowly and, in many instances, without vibrato. One added the vibrato as one became physically secure in the passage.

Mr Lasserson did not like a particularly big sound. This was startling to me , coming as I did from America where a big sound was always emphasised. However, I began to tone down my volume level and replaced some of the 'loud' with colour and softness

3

My lessons were fused with Lasserson's stories of his student days in Leopold Auer's class in St Petersburg. His memory of those days was remarkable, and I recall several events he shared with me. He described his summertime visit, with his classmate Mischa Elman, to the country house of Elman's cousin. The two young violinists would practice each morning across a hall from each other. Sascha recalled, "I could hear Elman playing every concerto he could, with his big golden sound, over a period of three to four hours. He just played through and never stopped to correct any inaccuracies. Meanwhile, I practised scales and études and passages from my concertos and pieces as Auer requested. Mischa and I were so different in the way we practised. I don't think he practised at all! He just played..."

In 1966 Elman came to London to see his friend and classmate Sascha, 'for help' on the Khachaturian concerto; Mr Lasserson told me this as he knew I loved the concerto. He also told me; "Mischa slows down in some of the tough passages, and then goes back into tempo." I know that Sascha loved Elman as a 'great talent', and their long friendship was interrupted only by Elman's death in 1967.

Lasserson told me that he had given the first performance in Russia of the Glazunov concerto, with the composer conducting – commenting, modestly, that "Glazunov liked my playing."

In reference to Auer, Lasserson had a limitless admiration for his teacher, and spoke of him with the greatest respect. He explained that he was truly Auer's assisting coach in St Petersburg because, as he put it, "Auer knew I could analyse technical problems, and solve them. He knew I was interested in the how of playing the violin."

From what I could gather, Leopold Auer had a very high regard for Sascha, and felt his knowledge and interest in building violin technique placed him in a pre-eminent position among all his famous classmates, including Heifetz, Seidel, Zimbalist, Elman, Piastro, Kathleen Parlow, Cecilia Hansen and, much later, Milstein

One evening I was invited to Mr and Mrs Lasserson's home for dinner. It was an amazing visit filled with stories of Russia and of colleagues who had studied with him. After coffee and dessert, Sascha brought out some remarkable documents, one of which was his diploma of graduation from the St Petersburg Conservatory, signed by Glazunov, and a member of the Royal Family. To my knowledge, Lasserson was the only pupil in that famous class of Leopold Auer actually to graduate and receive such a diploma.

The other documents he showed us (I was then married to an Oxford Mathematics graduate, John Roberts, who was a fine amateur violinist) were several letters of reference about Sascha as a great violinist and teacher, from Mischa Elman, Efrem Zimbalist, and Jascha Heifetz, hand-written by his illustrious colleagues to try to persuade him to come to New York to open a teaching studio. All had promised to help him establish himself as a principal violin pedagogue there.

4

However, Lasserson remained in London with his beloved wife, Zelda, who was also a distant cousin. They had two sons and, when I knew them, lived modestly in a three-bedroom flat in Ladbroke Grove. Lasserson was a very happy man, married to the woman he loved. Zelda was a quiet and dignified lady with a twinkle in her eye. She was entirely devoted to her husband, and believed completely in his unique gifts. Their union was such that

I believe it enabled Lasserson to be as benevolent and selfless as he was. It is quite possible that the love and moral support of his wife more than compensated for the lack of that world fame accorded to some of Sascha's classmates. I believe England gave Sascha his showcase because, when he arrived in London there were no great – or acknowledged as great – pedagogues armed with the Auer tradition of violin playing. A measure of this is the undoubted fact that much of the world-wide acclaim accorded to British orchestras up to 1978 (the year of Lasserson's passing) and beyond, and in particular to the string sound, is a direct reflection of Lasserson's impact on several generations of English violinists. Some of his greatest pupils have been orchestral leaders, including Rodney Friend and Trevor Williams. He also produced some great violin soloists, and one takes this opportunity to salute Tessa Robbins, for whom Sascha had a high musical regard and who has been passing on the Lasserson tradition in her teaching. Another disciple is Nona Liddell, who has taught the Lasserson method for many years to great effect.

5

There is another important aspect to Lasserson's artistry and pedagogy, and that is his connection with Nathan Milstein – musically, violinistically and culturally. Although he was at the tail-end of Lasserson's tenure in Auer's class, Milstein knew and revered Sascha Lasserson. I know this because Milstein once cleared a wall-to-wall group of backstage Festival Hall concertgoers from his dressing room the minute Sascha Lasserson set foot inside to say hello. Milstein and Lasserson hugged each other in Russian style, speaking rapidly in their mother tongue with obvious mutual delight. Then Lasserson did something almost unprecedented in teaching circles. He deliberately introduced me, his pupil, and insisted that Mr Milstein hear me play. The greatness of Mr Lasserson's gesture towards me, and his own self-strength, are even more poignant and moving to me as I write about this almost 28 years later. (One sees much in life, particularly when leaving the role of violin ingenue for the more transcendent one of seasoned player and pedagogue.) So far, I have yet to witness anything like the selflessness of that gesture in Milstein's dressing room, when the senior statesman of violin pedagogy, in effect, turned over a (by then) moulded young disciple to a great name and artist for a chance in the world game of 'Career.'

If I am anything of a witness to Lasserson and Milstein, I testify to many similarities in their approach to the bow, to the left hand, to their true love and regard for music and total lack of self-absorption. While I worked with Milstein, Lasserson was still my violin 'father' in England. He saw the growth in my awareness as imprinted by the Milstein imagination. There were no conflicts for me in all the three years of private study with Milstein because Lasserson's younger colleague mirrored and embellished all that Lasserson did and taught. England may not know this – but I do, because I was a blessed 'guinea-pig', as Milstein used to call me, his first really true private pupil in London.

It has been said that 'True greatness never reveals nor cherishes much ambition, for the gift of mind and the possession of a profound character leave little for the soul to wish or the Earth to care for.' (Rev David Swing, Chicago Central Church – Presbyterian, 1874).

The above quotation is a perfect description of Sascha Lasserson, and gives us the answer to why he needed so little external attention. Each new pupil offered Sascha a new life as a teacher, for he could tailor-make a technique to suit the individual but with the unmistakable stamp of Lasserson.

Thank you, Mr Lasserson, wherever you are – for you are living in the hands and hearts of my pupils in America, and further afield.

Elisabeth Matesky, a Fulbright scholar, studied with Sascha Lasserson (on Heifetz's recommendation) and later with Milstein (on Sascha's recommendation). She has been an awardee at the Sibelius Competition in Helsinki, an artist-teacher at the American Conservatory in Chicago, and has held teaching residencies at Trinity College London and the Sibelius Academy in

Helsinki. She played in the Chicago Symphony Orchestra under Solti and was a White House recitalist for President Carter and the French premier Raymond Barre. Now an international solo artist working in the USA and Europe, she has recorded the Brahms, Bruch, Sibelius, and Glazunov concerti – as well as the Vivaldi Double Concerto, with Henryk Szeryng.

Editor's Afterthought

As was pointed out in the introduction, Sascha's great contemporaries left huge discographies: their recordings have been issued and re-issued, with analytical notes and photographs galore. We know the Heifetz sound; we know the Elman sound. We know how Heifetz played Bach, how Elman played the Mendelssohn – we can listen as many times as we like. There are recordings of Milstein, of Seidel, of Zimbalist, of Polyakin; there is film footage, now available on video, so that the fable almost becomes flesh. But of Sascha there are only these memories: some photographs; some programmes; a tiny recorded fragment of a Dvorak Slavonic Dance – and nothing else

During the preparation of this book, however, there seemed some slight chance that we might find film footage of him because, in the late sixties, the BBC started work on a television documentary about two rising young stars in very different fields of endeavour. Elisabeth Matesky had, by then, commenced her studies with Sascha, and the phenomenal young athlete Lilian Board was achieving success. The idea was to discuss the dynamic that drove them on, each in her different way, and to compare the disciplines of practising and rehearsing, and athletic training. Each was filmed with teacher and trainer, so that Sascha was filmed in his studio.

Tragically, Lilian Board died very young. The BBC abandoned the project, and nobody thought to save the film. When I started work on this book, the idea that such film might still exist led me to phone all over BBCTV, starting with Humphrey Burton. Eventually a suggestion from Elisabeth Matesky led me to contact the writer Jamila Gavin. She, as Jamila Patten, had actually been involved in the making of the documentary and remembered it well. I have to thank her, for she joined enthusiastically in the search, actually tracking down the cameraman who had worked on the project. The search led, eventually, to the old Ealing Studios, but nothing could be found. The great men of another era are preserved for us - for example, Brahms' voice can be heard on a very old Edison cylinder; the painter Renoir is seen sitting in his garden, his brush making a minute arthritic arc as he struggles to put paint on canvas. But, in our time, with all that technology available – nobody thought, nobody remembered. And we missed Sascha.

Ann Measures

Dear, kind, inspiring, wonderfully intuitive Sascha Lasserson was about eighty-five years old when I first met him, just a few years before he died.

After several years of gruelling freelance playing I knew that my violin technique was woefully inadequate and my hands were stiff and painful. Convinced by the warm assurances of a friend, a former Lasserson pupil, I arrived at the Shepherds Bush studio in great trepidation. What possible interest could this great teacher, Leopold Auer's one-time assistant and Heifetz's classmate, have in such a pupil?

Short of stature, his keen eyes peering through his thick round glasses, he opened the door for me, cigarette in hand; and as he played me the first bars of Vieuxtemps' A minor Concerto I entered a completely different world. His clear, sweet sound was expressive and singing such as I had never heard before, and as I watched his gentle powerful hands moulding the sound, flexible unhurried fingers moving close to the strings, long left thumb continuously mobile, his sensitive right hand seemingly melded to the bow, my own hands seemed to lose some of their stiffness and began to understand.

At first he would mark my music for me, explaining briefly in his idiomatic Russian-tinged English the reason for a choice of fingering, or just where to save the bow, or how to achieve an articulation. Later on, however, he would stop me in mid-passage, by lifting my bow off the string with the tip of his bow to explain by playing rather than in words. This never felt doctrinaire, for he taught without any self-importance. He was simply showing the way into the music. In response to my cry that I had no technique he replied, "Technique!" (sounding the "ch" from the back of his throat). "What is technique? It is to play a beautiful note – to phrase beautifully, to make the music sing." But then he made everything sing.

He had a profound philosophy of life – "I always encourage my pupils," he would say, quietly finding something good and positive, so that one never felt too insignificant in this remarkable company. He gave real advice on how to work to improve memory; to build up repertoire; to develop flexibility of the left hand (he rescued my tight vibrato, sagely advising me to practise with none, at the same time softening my left wrist and methodically training the independence of the fingers) and to use the bow expressively.

"There is always time," he would say, showing how to play a fast passage by practising it very slowly, whilst preparing each next finger ahead. In these lessons, observing how he worked, I really began to understand how to practise.

He taught ways of practising scales: G major in 4 octaves was asked for at each lesson ("to achieve speed start slowly like a runner"); scales in 2 octaves on one string; scales in broken thirds; 4-octave arpeggio passages based on one in *Symphonie Espagnole*. Double scales received special care: in double thirds the intervals were to be changed one finger at a time, each pair of fingers then swapping strings in the quest for flexibility and perfect intonation. He paid much attention to the left thumb not pressing sideways on the neck, and pointing it slightly backwards when moving into high positions to facilitate bringing the hand round. He devised a special exercise to develop flexibility and independence of the left hand in which the 4th finger is placed on the E string on top C, the 2nd on C on the A string, the 1st on Eb on the D string, and the 3rd then plays on each string moving chromatically.

One day he told a story which amused him very much, to illustrate how to practise (and how not to be concerned by what others might think): the window-cleaner had come into the room where Sascha was practising thirds – slow, quiet sounds without vibrato – and enquired sarcastically of the old man how long he had been playing the violin! Another time he recounted hearing Kreisler

Fig 1 Paganini Caprice No. 1

Fig 2 Vieuxtemps A minor concerto

Fig 3 Wienawski Concerto No. 2 in D minor

practising whilst on tour (in Scarborough, I think) – just little strange sounds emerging from behind the stage door – demonstrating economy and concentration in good practice.

The Kreutzer studies were the source of basic skills. He directed me to No.1 for long sustained bows with light fluid passage-work; to No.4 for staccato – tiny inflections of fingers and thumb with the stick turned, slowly at first then with double notes, fitting the left hand to the right, both up-bow and down. Similarly in No.7 Martele was to be practised slowly, the sharp, small accents followed by a quiet, gentle tone, with much attention paid to the release of pressure and the preparation of the next note. No. 9 was used for finger independence and intonation, stopping though not sounding the octaves throughout. Recommended too were No. 11 for ease and expressiveness of shifting and No.13 with every imaginable variation of bowing, the elbow moving the whole arm with the shape of the passage ... and thence to the Bach E major Prelude. No.32 and the other double-stopping studies were also a preparation for Bach.

Lasserson regarded the true nature of the violin to be based on the cantabile and virtuoso repertoire of the great 19th-century players so many of whom he had heard. The only way to learn to play was to study their music. He taught with his violin in his hand and showed exactly how to tackle seemingly impossible feats; for example, in Paganini Caprice No.1 how to spread the left hand helping with the thumb, where to release fingers, and how to follow the curve of the bridge with the bow, holding firmly as if playing staccato to make the bow jump. In No.5 (see fig.1) he showed how to play fast semiquavers: "Don't try to make the bow jump; keep it on the string and it will sound off". Caprice No.10 he played most expressively, demonstrating how to articulate each note in the up-bows with his supple fingers on the stick.

It was not so much in studies as in the repertoire, however, that Lasserson imparted his wonderful knowledge and love of the violin. In the Vieuxtemps A minor Concerto (fig.2) he showed me how to move around the fingerboard, how to use the bow, how to choose expressive fingerings, how to play the style of this music which he himself had learned at the age of twelve from Galkin, a pupil of Vieuxtemps.

Wieniawski was Violinist to the Tsar and Professor of Violin in St Petersburg for twelve years before Leopold Auer was appointed. The influence of his virtuosic playing was enormous and Lasserson knew well how the gymnastics and beautiful melodies of his Concerto No.2 in D minor should be played (fig.3), demonstrating it all by memory as he played everything else.

The Brahms Concerto was written for Joachim, who taught Leopold Auer. It seemed at first unplayable, yet Mr Lasserson showed how to work at it. For example, in the development, at bar 304, he interpreted the double-stopped theme most poignantly with very little vibrato, and the *leggiero ma espressivo* he bowed with great delicacy and a melancholy not usually heard today. In the slow movement, too, his legato fingerings and seamless bowings had a restraint and integrity with less vibrato than is now fashionable.

Tchaikovsky dedicated his Violin Concerto to Auer, and Lasserson conveyed its poetry and its Russian character as he explained its technical demands. He described how he heard Auer performing all the violin solos in the Tchaikovsky ballets at the Kirov Theatre in his role as Imperial Court Violinist, where he also played, for example, Drigo's *Waltz Bluette* and Tchaikovsky's *Melodie* op.42 – with a different ending from the printed one, which Sascha showed me.

The Glazunov Concerto is closely associated with Sascha Lasserson since he played it with the composer conducting on tour in the Russian provinces. Hearing his expressive portamento, his long melancholy phrasing at the opening and his agility in the cadenza, conveyed to me the breadth and richness of the tradition with which he was connected.

In the classical literature, the Beethoven Concerto held a special place in his teaching. Here, he played with a most noble and pure tone and, with his keen ear, he focused on the discipline needed in this work – for example, insisting on Viotti bowing in the thirteenth bar of the second solo entry.

A Bach fugue, he said, should be practised every day to develop tone, not crashing but drawing the bow through the chords. He taught solo Bach with his customary detailed attention to the rhythmic structure, always indicating which part of the bow to use, and which notes to bring out. In Bach he had such beautiful phrasing and a lively but gentle bow.

He had a special idea that the Prelude of the G minor Sonata had been inspired by Bach hearing a Cantor singing in the synagogue, and it should be played like a fantasy – but only after practising it counting 16 in every bar. To assist in memorising he advised me always to practise Bach from the music – in this way, he said, the memory would last longer.

Achron's *Hebrew Melody* was very close to Lasserson's heart. He asked if I knew it and gave me a photocopy of the music, which he played so movingly. He was apparently very fond of Achron, describing how he saw his fellow classmate one day walking down the corridor in the Conservatoire in St Petersburg aged about 10 and muttering to himself. As Sascha passed him he was overheard repeating, "F major – one flat, G major – one sharp – but poor C major hasn't got anything, poor C major!" He often spoke of his fellow students almost as if he still lived in that far-off world and if I mentioned a violin performance I'd heard he would listen with interest then shake his head and say, "Me you cannot astonish!" Sometimes, when teaching at his flat in North Kensington, Mr Lasserson would point to a large photograph of his class and name all the great players: Zimbalist, Toscha Seidl, Piastro, Achron, Cecilia Hansen, Milstein, and Heifetz, seen as young students grouped around their Professor. He would recall their playing, and how sternly Auer taught the class. He also referred to Auer's own St Petersburg Quartet, observing that it needs the finest players to play chamber music and that it is not enough to be a good musician without technical skill.

Leopold Auer must have been a father-figure to his class, both loved and respected and held in awe. One day, after a concert, he invited his pupils to dinner and served lobster. This put Sascha in a difficult position since, as a Jew, he did not wish to eat the lobster and described to me how he solved the problem by hiding his food in a plant pot. Sascha suddenly seemed like a conspiratorial schoolboy as he told the story, and this quality of naïve simplicity was part of his greatness. By chance, my lesson was the first he gave when he resumed work after his wife's death (about a year before he died), and, as I offered my sympathy, he wept, saying simply, "You see, I loved my wife – we were married for sixty years and now I talk to her and she isn't there."

He had such warmth and deep understanding of people, encouraging his pupils over and over again to be optimistic, to "keep practising" and with enjoyment so that even though not reaching the top they would have the reward of the music. His great integrity led him to remain independent of any conservatoire in England so that he had regard only for his own standards and each pupil's needs irrespective of his reputation or financial gain. His lifestyle was modest and he was extremely generous, charging very low fees.

But he had a great sense of humour, too, delighting in the tricks he imparted to overcome difficulties in Sarasate's *Zapateado* and chuckling over a past pupil who complained that there were 'wrong notes' on the last page of the *Rondo Capriccioso* (11 bars from the end). There were several passages he enjoyed asking for out of the blue; he had a special fingering for the fourth bar of *Zigeunerweisen* (4, 4-4 harmonic) at the top, and he mischievously told how he challenged Heifetz with it backstage at the Albert Hall after a concert.

Zigeunerweisen

Fig 4

At the end of every lesson he was sure to ask, peering at the music stand, "Got all the music?" following it with, "You know what to do?" And sometimes as you replied, "Yes, Mr Lasserson," he would grin and add, "Well why don't you do it?"

Ann Measures, freelance musician; has played in opera and ballet, and with BBC orchestras. She met Sascha Lasserson when he was 85, and studied with him for three years. She now teaches and plays chamber music.

Miriam Morris

My first memories of 'Uncle' Sascha are from my early childhood when he would visit us in Manchester. I remember him as a small, gentle, chain-smoking man with a heavy Russian accent who was totally preoccupied with the violin. He would often play, sometimes accompanied by my mother, who was a pupil of Solomon. The opening of the E major Bach Partita is something that I remember in particular. My father was an amateur violinist, self-taught in his adult years who, much to Sascha's annoyance, doggedly refused any guidance in terms of the purchase of a suitable instrument and the odd lesson.

We moved to London when I was seven. Sascha offered to teach me the violin. He lent me a small fractional-sized instrument which I believe he had played in his youth. I remember going to his modest flat in Ladbroke Grove for my beginner lessons. This was indeed a privilege of which I was blissfully unaware! Maybe if I had understood Sascha's accent, I would have made better progress. I have clear recollections of his frustration with me, knocking my bow off the string when I failed to comprehend his words of wisdom. I met my Waterloo with vibrato, after which the lessons ceased. I have no doubt that the relief was mutual.

The violin had always felt much more comfortable to me played like a cello. When I subsequently started the cello at boarding school I knew I had found my instrument. Naturally, I was summoned to play to Sascha when I came home for the school holidays. To this day, I can remember the horror in his expression and voice when he said, "Get her to a doctor quickly!" I did find my cello doctor in the fine cellist John Shinebourne. I played to Sascha frequently in my student days. By this time I was sufficiently mature to be able to understand and value his advice.

As the doyen of the Russian school of violin teaching in Europe,

Sascha would hold court at Festival Hall when the virtuoso Russian violinists and cellists came to play in London. As a little girl, I would be taken along and I would meet these luminaries. In particular, I have vivid memories of him introducing me to Milstein and Rostropovich. I remember being told to sit quietly in a corner of the artists' room at Festival Hall whilst Milstein and Sascha had a lengthy post mortem on the concerto he had just performed, after which the public were allowed to enter. Such was Sascha's humility, however, that, some years later, when Heifetz was booked to make a rare appearance in London, I was amazed to meet him queuing for a ticket to hear his friend and colleague. Sadly, Heifetz did not fulfil that engagement.

Sascha taught many of the foremost violinists in post-war England. It would have been perfectly feasible for a man of his stature to have been selective in his choice of students and to charge high fees. However, this was not his way. I remember, as a student, being asked to play in a quartet. Both violinists were pupils of Sascha. Their regard and affection for him was enormous and his influence was obvious. They were serious students but with a modest capacity. Over the years I have come across various rank and file violinists who are grateful for their time with Sascha, remembering with gratitude his ability to sort out their particular problems. He was a teacher of the utmost integrity, and for this, above all, he should be remembered.

Miriam Morris began as a cellist, studying with John Shinebourne, and then switched to Viola da Gamba, which she studied with Wieland Kuijken. She now lives and works in Australia, where she is one of the country's leading influences in the field of period instrument performance. She has had a varied career as a soloist, chamber musician, continuo and orchestral player. She teaches cello and viola da gamba at Melbourne University and created the current cello syllabus for the Australian Music Examination Board, together with a companion technical work book for cello (published by Allen's, Australia).

Robin Morrish

On the recommendation of another of Sascha's pupils, I had the good fortune to study with the Russian teacher from 1961-1972, travelling up to his first-floor studio in Ladbroke Grove on a fortnightly basis. I was often his last pupil in the afternoon, and the lesson invariably stretched well beyond the hour for the modest fee of £3, which he eventually raised to £4.50 in 1970.

Although small in stature, Sascha never found it necessary to convey the impression of the great imposing professor. His authority was of the gentle, persuasive kind, commanding respect through the integrity of his technique and musicianship.

As is well known, Sascha was a chain-smoker and often the cigarette ash would fall inside his (or my!) violin through the f-holes and my instrument would carry the smell for days following. On one occasion, in the early days of my lessons, I brought my parents to meet him and thereafter at the end of every lesson he would say farewell with "And remember me to your father."

Lessons always began with a four-octave scale and arpeggio, except on certain occasions in the winter when he would say that it was too cold for scales! But, as long as they were done, it did not matter when; the end of a practice session was as beneficial as the beginning! He always insisted on good intonation and I can hear him now saying, "Tune your violin," at regular intervals through the lesson; also, the smoothness of execution, working constantly on shifting and the bow change.

Not surprisingly, he considered the Russian school of violin playing, style and technique to be pre-eminent and he didn't have much of a good word to say for the others. He claimed that a pupil of the Russian style had unique qualities which marked him out from all others – the particular hallmark of such a player was to be recognised by his VIBRATO. Sascha was most insistent in his teaching of this, advocating the small oscillation varying in speed and intensity but not in size. He especially warned against excessive vibrato on the upper register of the E string, and he would urge no vibrato when practising intonation accuracy.

He regarded double-stopping in octaves and thirds as the finest technical practice for the left hand, and felt that up and down-bow staccato was essentially a trick, a knack. Some otherwise fine violinists with advanced techniques cannot do it, while other – more indifferent – players just have the knack, regardless of other technical achievements. He would also advise, in addition to scales, practising arpeggio sequences and elaborations – as in broken chords thus:

and minor figurations to practise close semitones for intonation, with large left hand fingers, thus:

Another exercise was that of broken thirds in B flat and B major – two octaves in one bow.

Sascha remained on the outside of the mainstream of teaching going on at the colleges in London. He would speak wistfully of pupils who had come from these institutions to play the Sibelius or Brahms Concerto to him and then were unable to play the four-octave scale of G major he requested!

He had much to say about style and good taste. At that time there was the new vogue of 'correct' playing in baroque music and the early classical period. But Sascha would say that good 'taste' should prevail in all violin playing. It was as important to play the Tchaikovsky Concerto with a sense of refinement as a Handel Sonata. When it came to the Beethoven Concerto I remember him emphasising that a clearly defined, firm tradition as to its performance and interpretation had grown up over the years and that a violinist strayed outside those limits at his peril.

He regarded the Bach solo sonatas and the Paganini Caprices as the Old and New Testaments of the violinist's bible, and would speak of the Jewish tradition behind Bach's music – based on his idea that Bach had heard the singing of a cantor in the synagogue, and that we could hear such influence in the Prelude of the first Solo Sonata.

Again, it could be heard in the keening lament figuration of the accented passing note, as in 'Erbarme Dich' in the St Matthew Passion.

Sascha would often refer to the old days back in Russia, which he naturally held in pride and affection. He told me how he was in the Leopold Auer class alongside Jascha Heifetz. Auer commented on one occasion, "I see which way the future is going for you two: you, Jascha, will become the player, but you, Sascha, will be the teacher."

My own experience of the quality of Sascha's teaching may be summed up in the following incident: I arrived late one afternoon for my lesson to find Trevor Williams having a final lesson of a series with Sascha. I was asked to sit and wait in the corner for them to finish. They were deeply immersed in the study of the cadenza in the first movement of the Tchaikovsky Concerto. When they had concluded their discussion and playing, Trevor Williams presented Sascha with a gift – a hand-written letter and signature from Joseph Joachim. Sascha was immensely delighted with this and kept taking it out of his pocket and reading it over again after Trevor had left, saying to me how absolutely thrilled he was with it. But when my lesson started, Sascha was immediately as immersed in concentration and undivided attention on my G major scale as he had been before with the Tchaikovsky cadenza.

One of the works Sascha strongly encouraged me to study was the Glazunov Concerto. He had a particularly close association with this work because he had performed it in Russia with the composer himself conducting. I therefore felt a sense of a direct line of communication straight from the source as I studied this concerto with Sascha. I remember too the time when I brought the first violin part of the Mendelssohn Octet which I had bowed and fingered for myself. It met with his approval and he said I had now grasped the principles for myself which he had been trying to inculcate. An example of such would be: to shift at the semi-tone wherever possible; or to avoid bow-changing in legato at a string-crossing.

Even in his later years, Sascha's technique remained secure and impressive, together with his memory. I shall never forget the occasion when he picked up his fiddle (cigarette in mouth, of course!) and launched into a magnificent account of Wilhelm Ernst's Variations on *The Last Rose of Summer*. Auer was right that Sascha was the born teacher, but there was no doubt that he could play also alongside the greatest of his colleagues in the violin world.

How fortunate for us violinists in Britain that – after the Exodus from Russia in 1917, when so many of the great Leopold Auer pupils fled across the Atlantic to America – Sascha Lasserson should have chosen to curtail his westward journey and settle in London, to give immeasurable service to generations of younger violinists here who have thus been enabled to carry on the torch of the great Auer tradition.

Robin Morrish was a member of the Choral Society at King's College, Cambridge, where he read English and Classics. He studied with Sascha Lasserson for twelve years before going on to teach at King's Canterbury, and then Marlborough. Then he moved to become Head of Strings at Tonbridge. He led the Edinburgh Rehearsal Orchestra as well as several other orchestras in southern England. Recently he retired from his post at Tonbridge.

Peter Mountain

Sascha's teaching was based on positive logic, a simple and direct approach and, above all, kindness and sympathy. The positive approach meant that, instead of finding faults in one's playing and trying to correct them, he seemed to find the good points and worked to build on them. Previously I had often been told not to do this and that – not to stiffen the bowing arm, not to phrase in such and such a way. Sascha always said, "This is good – now do this – you see, it is better!"

His insistence on purity of intonation was memorable. The exercises he gave were simple and basic, but immensely helpful if practised properly. I remember them well and try to pass them on to pupils. Thirds, slowly built up with no vibrato and super-critical listening were asked for at most lessons. Also, slow bowing exercises with controlled and even crescendo and diminuendo were the basis of his right arm teaching.

He was the only person who had ever clearly and concisely described to me the balance and control of the bow. Maybe others had talked about such things before, but when Sascha said anything, in his quiet and knowledgeable way, you remembered it. Like all great teachers he was always confident that what he said was right, but he was also very modest. He would say, "All this I tell you is not mine – it is just what I learned from Auer." But he would not add that which we knew, that he had the wonderful gift of being able to impart it to others.

His gifts and talent as a player were truly impressive. I had first heard about him from my wife, who was playing as a pianist and accompanist for CEMA concerts for troops and factory workers at the end of the war. She talked about this wonderful little Russian violinist, playing with fantastic technique and most lovely sound, but a rather shy and gentle person, so that he often ended up with his back to the audience! The piece she particularly remembers is the beautiful Tchaikovsky *Melodie* from Op. 42. He was also always losing his hat, and Angela had to mother him between concerts!

Sascha did not have the kind of personality to revel in public performance, but he did have all the technical and musical attributes of a great player. And, even without a showy presentation, whenever he started to play, everyone listened! He must have been the equal, and at the same time the opposite, of Mischa Elman, his childhood friend and fellow pupil of Leopold Auer. He talked about Elman with admiration, but sometimes suggested that the playing which made Mischa a world-famous star was not always in the best of taste! On the other hand, his admiration for Heifetz was unreserved. He told lovely stories about returning as a senior student to Auer's class to hear this phenomenal little boy of ten playing the Ernst concerto to a stunned gathering. After little Jascha had finished, Auer said, "Well, who will play now?" Excuses came thick and fast – one student had not prepared anything suitable, another had a cold, another's violin was not in good order. Eventually, one from the back of the class (not the most talented!) said loudly, "I'll play." Auer retorted smartly, "Oh no, we don't want to hear you!"

Heifetz always showed his admiration and affection for Sascha, and would meet him every time he came to London. There is a beautiful photograph, showing the two of them together, looking appreciatively at a fine violin.

His musical memory was phenomenal. Naturally it embraced all the standard violin repertoire, but Sascha was quick to explore new works and equally quick to memorise them and to be able to help others with them. I remember studying the Khachaturian Concerto with him when it was relatively new to Britain. With Sascha's guidance, it taught me so much about finding the best fingering through thinking enharmonically. His memory was no doubt enhanced by necessity, as his eyesight was poor. During the war years and after, when he was not well known and his income was low, his advanced students tried to get him a few orchestral dates. At the first rehearsal he would be hopelessly lost most of the time, peering through thick glasses at (to him) unfamiliar orchestral parts. But he would always take the music home and next day would play perfectly, having memorised the entire programme!

One of Sascha's greatest qualities as a teacher was his ability to make students think for themselves. There are teachers who foster a sense of dependence in pupils, so that they can find difficulty in making decisions without the approval and help of the authoritative father-figure. Sascha understood that, in the end, the only real teachers are the individual players themselves. The teacher's job is to direct them how to practise, how to think independently, how to think positively and, in the end, how to launch themselves as individual artists. His gift was to make us aware of the truths we had learned, and to realise that we should be grateful to inherit the accumulated wisdom of great players and teachers of the past.

Sascha loved to talk and chat about all aspects of the violin, sharing with us his memories of players and performances so that lessons came alive with a sense of achievement and of belonging to a great living tradition. He once said a surprising thing: we were talking about Kreisler and I asked rather naively what was the great thing about Kreisler which raised him so high? His immediate reply was, "Kreisler had the greatest technique of all!" A very surprising opinion – we young players at the time had been brought up to consider Heifetz as the greatest technician, and to revere Kreisler as the supreme master of creative interpretation, rubato and unique tonal beauty, though perhaps not always infallible in technical accuracy. Sascha immediately explained with words which epitomised his whole violinistic philosophy. This was the general sense of it:

To produce the phrasing, the subtlety, the nuance and control of truly great playing you need technique. It is not sufficient just to think beautiful thoughts; you must know how to express them, how to play in such a way that the beauty of the music is communicated to the listener. Technique is not merely playing in tune, in time, accurately, fast, mechanically better than others. There is much, much more to it than mere athleticism. Of course it is necessary to train the hands, the arms, the body to be able physically to cope with the incredibly complex reactions needed to play the violin. But this is only the beginning and should never be divorced from the musical ends. What are we playing the violin for? Are we mere circus performers, dazzling others with technical skills or are we not surely re-creators of the composers' inspired thoughts? To be able to attempt that high aim requires not only insight into the music's ideal shape and meaning but also the physical skill to make these ideas clear in performance.

My father, who taught me violin in the early days, had a story of the great actress Ellen Terry, who was complimented on the climactic scene in a particular play where she rushed across the stage, flinging herself, sobbing, onto a couch. Her reply was that she always had to remember to start from offstage on her left foot, then twelve paces across to the couch, as it was essential that she arrived there on her right foot so that the final fall didn't look awkward and ridiculous. A perfect example of the art which conceals art; the technique needed to produce a carefully thought-out artistic effect. Sascha never let us forget the interdependence of technical perfection and musical creativeness. To that end he rarely asked for many actual studies to be prepared. We had to do his own basic technical exercises and scales, as I have mentioned before, but by far the greatest part of the teaching was based on actual repertoire. Pianists have the great advantage of being able to work on studies and etudes written by Chopin, Schumann, Liszt, Brahms, Rachmaninov and so on. We as violinists are not so fortunate. The studies of Kreutzer, though admirable in many ways, are not musically stimulating. Sascha knew that it is important for young players to be given musical problems to solve and not be allowed to focus exclusively on merely mechanical achievements.

He would often demonstrate at lessons, and his playing was as instructive and inspirational as his words. The *piu animato* semiquaver passage in the first movement of the Glazunov Concerto (one of his favourites) was in Sascha's hands dazzling. I have never head it more sparkling, more accurate, but at the same time more beautifully shaped. Another similar passage where he gave me tremendous help was the 2nd Variation in the slow movement of Beethoven's *Kreutzer* Sonata which also features alternate staccato and legato at high speed. Sascha helped with the bowing skills needed, but also suggested specific points of rubato which had to be clearly practised. He insisted it was not enough to leave it to the inspiration of the movement, although the finished performance must sound perfectly spontaneous.

Much is talked in these days about performances that are 'old-fashioned', as if to say that we now have arrived at a pinnacle of perfection from which we look down on the past with disdain. Never forget that in a couple of generations our present standards will be superseded by other changing ideals. Music performance is a living art which evolves with the changing culture of our society. We can learn from the generous portamenti of Kreisler and others which we can hear in early recordings, without having to copy them parrot-fashion. The only thing that remains a constant factor is 'taste'. Styles of playing vary, today more than ever, with the newer ideas of period performance often rather pointlessly creating a battleground between different schools of thought. The truth is surely that all approaches, if sincere and sensitive, are valid and that the one can learn from the other. A tasteless performance of a Bach Partita, either by a traditional player (for want of a better word) or one who has all the equipment and knowledge of Baroque performing styles, will be offensive and non-satisfying, while either kind of presentation, artistically done, is worthy of praise. Shakespeare can be performed in modern dress, or as it was originally seen and heard in the Globe Theatre, and with an open mind you can enjoy both.

But what is taste, you may ask? That certainly is the question, to which there is no definite answer and there never will be. The only way we can develop 'taste' is by the example of the greatest amongst us – people like Sascha who have not only the knowledge and the experience handed down from others, but also the instinct to know what is good and musically truthful.

I have spoken earlier about Sascha's reverence for the memory of Leopold Auer, and his modesty regarding his own contributions. But it is obvious that in a long life he had modified these memories and evolved his own style of playing as well as creating his own school of teaching. In comparison to Carl Flesch, the other great violin pedagogue of the early 20th century, Auer has left a modest amount of written description of his teaching methods, and we certainly learnt far more from Sascha than can be found in *Violin Playing As I Teach It*, which Auer produced in 1921. One notable advance was even admitted by Sascha when he told us that Auer considered the violin concertos of J. S. Bach not to be worth studying, being dull and without technical challenge! He certainly did not agree with his old teacher there, and these marvellous works found a regular place in the repertoire for his pupils.

However, it must be said that Auer produced probably a more illustrious number of great violinists than any other pedagogue this century, and Sascha was an eminent and loyal member of that great body. One final anecdote might be used as illustration. In the early 1950s David Oistrakh made his first visit to England, performing and recording with the Philharmonia Orchestra of which I was then a member. Several others of the violin section were going to Sascha for lessons at the time and we all gave him glowing accounts of this fantastic virtuoso. Oistrakh was to do a broadcast of the Tchaikovsky Concerto from Maida Vale studios with the BBC Symphony Orchestra and I managed to get invited-audience tickets. Being for the first time the proud owner of a car, I invited Sascha to use one of my tickets and took him along. It was a wonderful performance and nobody could fail to be impressed. I awaited Sascha's verdict with real interest and the earnestness and idealism of youth – "What do you think, Sascha?" With his little quizzical smile and a determination to make his point he replied, "What a marvellous player he would have been if he had learnt with Auer!"

Peter Mountain studied first at the RCM with Rowsby Woof and then Frederick Grinke. He studied with Sascha Lasserson after war service. He was a member of the Boyd Neel and Philharmonia Orchestras, led the London Harpsichord Ensemble and the Royal Liverpool Philharmonic, and was concertmaster of the BBC Training Orchestra. He was guest-leader of many other orchestras in the UK, Head of Strings at the Scottish Academy of Music and Drama and String Coach for the NYO. An adjudicator and conductor, he was a regular broadcaster as a concerto-soloist, and as a sonata-duo with his wife, Angela Dale.

Sascha on his eightieth birthday.

LEOPOLD AUER AND HIS PUPILS This photograph, so familiar to all Sascha's pupils, had pride of place on his piano. At some time he must have described it to most, if not all of them. I remember it so well as a young boy, but to my shame I never asked my uncle to tell me who all these people were. The preparation of this book, however, prompted an attempt at identification.

We knew Sascha was sitting on the floor in the front row second from the left. Auer, of course, was in the centre of the second row. We questioned many of Sascha's pupils, but all too often they were unable to help with further identification. Tully Potter trawled his extensive archives, and we studied the photographic archives of The Strad where – other than Elman in a sailor

suit, aged five – the photographs were of adults, whereas the faces in the class photograph were of much younger people. To some extent, therefore, it became an exercise in facial forecasting, helped a little by exploring the internet, and we reached the following conclusions:

Elman sits on Sascha's left in the front row; next to him is Arnold Spiegler (much thanks to Peter Mountain for this identification) – and at the end of that row sits the very young Cecilia Hansen. Behind Sascha sits Kathleen Parlow. Behind Auer stands Isolde Menges, and behind and to her left stands Efrem Zimbalist. Other great talents in the class who may well have been present, included Burgin, Piastro, Seidel, Polyakin, Achron and Sascha's great friend, Anton Maskoff.

Opposite page: Sascha – teaching and talking.
This page (above): Sascha with Heifetz and (below) with his wife and Tessa Robbins at the Royal Albert Hall after her performance of the Mendelssohn Concerto in a BBC Promenade Concert.

WIGMORE HALL

WIGMORE STREET, W.1

SATURDAY
OCT.
27
AT
8.15

AT THE PIANO:
HAROLD CRAXTON

CHAPPELL
GRAND
PIANOFORTE

SASCHA LASSERSON
Violin Recital

TICKETS (inc. Tax) - 10/6, 5/9 & 3/-

From Mr. Sascha Lasserson, 59 St. Quintin Avenue, North Kensington, W.10
and at the Box Office, Wigmore Hall.

Opposite page (above): Poster for one of Sascha's recitals.
and (below) two photographs of Sascha as a young man.
This page: Glazunov, inscribed: 'To the Conservatoire prize winner Sascha
Lasserson for remembrance from Professor Glazunov.'

Above: Sascha's brother Semeon and his sister, Anna.
Below: Sascha with a young pupil, Jonathan Pritchard.

Norman Nelson

I am sure that most of my friends and colleagues writing here of their reminiscences of Mr Lasserson will have sharper memories than my own and will enjoy greater recall of their time spent with him. I can, however, talk a little about the major changes he made to my basic technique in general and, particularly, to my left hand and wrist. Some of these issues may interest students of violin pedagogy.

Mine was the 'gorilla' approach to violin playing, and I paid a high price, in terms of physical discomfort and mental tension, for any successes I might have had playing in the London orchestras of that time. Without doubt the foremost influence Mr Lasserson had on my overall playing abilities was the restructuring of the left arm, concentrating on straightening the wrist – which I held at an angle of approximately 45° – and insisting that the fingers do not induce the slightest tension or tightness in it. This unbending of the wrist was indeed a radical change of direction for me, for it meant that I had to rethink the whole business of the angle each finger made in its relation to the fingerboard. All the fingers had to incline backwards from the point of contact; from the more upright position where each first joint was more or less rigid and acting as a pivot. This allowed, in fact produced, greater flexibility of each joint, but more vitally the first. I think that this was the first time that I could see a faint hope of being able to control the width and speed of my vibrato.

One of the many lasting memories of Mr Lasserson's playing was that of the clean articulation of his fingerwork. He would demonstrate, over and over again, the crucial difference between the 'noise' of the fingers hitting and pressing the fingerboards (mine were the loudest on record) and the 'click', as it were, of the fingers hitting the string and essentially independent of any wrist involvement, as I have mentioned. My lessons with him at his home started, for the most part, rather early in the day and it was comfortingly obvious that he needed a little time for his fingers to warm up and for the characteristic click to announce itself. He set me the Paganini Caprice No.6 to study, with the aim of isolating the wrist. This refined greatly my appreciation of how minimal the pressure required of the fingers is in order to produce a true and clear tone. It has been with absolute confidence that I have passed on his advice to my students to this day – gorillas and quasi-gorillas alike. In the context of the above, it is fascinating to observe the demonstration photographs of Mr Lasserson's teacher, Leopold Auer, in his *Graded Course of Violin Playing, Part One*. The text accompanying the photos showing the preferred angles of both wrists leaves us in no doubt that possibly the greatest pedagogue in the history of violin playing favoured an angle approaching 45° for each wrist. This *Outline of Violin Study* – eight books, from the Preparatory to the Virtuoso grade – is exhaustive. Published in New York in 1926, four years before the death of Mr Auer, and when the great man was in his 81st year, it would suggest that he maintained his theory of bent wrists throughout the whole course of his long teaching and playing career. As it is still readily available to teachers, at least throughout the North American continent, one can only presume that beginner students at the present time are still being urged to follow the bent wrist path – a path which the vast majority of today's professional violinists have chosen to ignore.

Mr Lasserson suggested that I approach troublesome runs backwards as it were. That is to say, making the elbow, wrist and especially the fingers relaxed and comfortable at the highest point of the run and then reversing the notes. This provided for a period of stillness when the fingertips could find their lightest touch on the strings, when this touch-sensation could best be memorised, and more easily anticipated when the passage was attempted the way it was written. All too often I had found myself on the concert platform and in the considerable heat of battle, applying far more pressure on the fingerboard than was good for me, to say nothing of the audience.

Whilst we are on the subject of finger pressure, I would like to mention a little advice generously directed my way by the universally revered violinist Joseph Szigeti. The London Symphony Orchestra was accompanying this unique artist on the occasion of what were to be his last recordings in England. During the interval of one of the sessions working on the Brahms concerto, I found myself still in my seat quietly practising something or other. Mr Szigeti, sitting eating an apple not far from me, called me over. He offered up his left hand and invited me to press down on the fingertips. There seemed to be no substance or firmness to them; rather like the feel of the fingers after a long hot soak in the tub. The flesh appeared to retreat and evaporate and I remember waiting with puzzlement for a response. I hope to remember for a long time yet what he said. His exact words were: "That is the result of a lifetime of wrong playing – don't press, my boy." Priceless advice from an extraordinarily honest and humble man and, as such, certainly reinforcing Mr Lasserson's teaching. And today, when I find myself in difficulties, I think back to that magical moment, and to the wonderful hours I spent hoping to soak up all the wisdom dear Mr Lasserson was doing his best to get into my mind. Dear, generous, caring Mr Lasserson; we all owe him an incalculable debt of gratitude. "Don't press, don't press!!" – there's hope for me still ...

Norman Nelson studied at the RCM before going to Sascha Lasserson, with whom he studied for a number of years. He was assistant Concertmaster of the LSO, RPO and BBC Symphony Orchestras and a founding member of the Academy of St Martin-in-the-Fields. In 1965 he was appointed Concertmaster of the Vancouver Symphony Orchestra, and founded the Purcell String Quartet there in 1969. He was appointed Professor of Violin and Chamber Music at University of Alberta in 1979. Now living on the west coast of British Columbia, he remains active as player, teacher and conductor.

Bernard Newland

I feel very privileged to have had periods of study with Sascha Lasserson. The lessons were always a great pleasure and of enormous interest. He gave you that wonderful feeling that you could play better than you thought you were able to play – one of the greatest assets of any teacher. Sascha would always demonstrate how various virtuosi would play certain passages.

His teaching was clear and direct, and he passed on that inspiring knowledge of the violin repertoire inherited from the wonderful traditions of the Auer School at St Petersburg. There, of course, he knew so many of the great violinists – including his great friend Jascha Heifetz.

Heifetz greatly valued Sascha's criticism of his playing, and was always far more concerned with what Sascha said rather than the critics. Sascha always came to his recording sessions.

He was a person of total integrity, devoted to his work and wonderfully kind.

Bernard Newland is a chamber and orchestral musician, who studied with Sascha Lasserson. He taught in the Junior Department of the RCM.

George Newman

Sascha was much more than a great teacher. He embodied cultural Russia of a by-gone age with special emphasis on its great music. In St Petersburg he had been a pupil of Leopold Auer, and whenever Sascha picked up his violin to illustrate a point, one was immediately transported back to the beautiful, romantic style and tone colour of the old school.

Sascha was very generous. When I started with him in 1948, he charged one guinea, and when I left after about five years, the fee was only thirty shillings! He regularly gave me more than an hour if there was no pupil following. He loved teaching and regarded it as a vocation, and not merely as a vehicle for making money. His great humanity, his understanding and gentleness showed itself in the care which he bestowed on his pupils.

Sascha once said to me that there is nothing more wonderful in life than to play chamber music with old friends. How I agree with him.

Sascha was not a pedagogic dictator. The choice of pieces was the result of mutual agreement. Perhaps the student's journey through the violin repertoire was sometimes less than structured, but it was more than richly rewarded by the encouragement to play the masterpieces of a half-forgotten repertoire.

Sascha taught by example – always standing and always his violin intervening effectively. Occasionally he would place his hand on my left hand to stop me in the middle of a phrase and, with its softness and flexibility, it communicated his great technique.

If Sascha wanted to refer to his own music, he searched through a huge pile which was on top of the piano, and of course the copy in question was usually at the bottom. When I was studying the *Rondo Capriccioso*, Sascha put in the orchestral parts on the violin. On another occasion he played to me the entire opening movement of the first Bach Solo Sonata.

When the Leningrad Philharmonic Orchestra first came to London, word got round in the violin section that Sascha was sitting near the front. Various players smiled and acknowledged him. After all, he had been in the same school as Heifetz, Zimbalist and Elman.

In the Tchaikovsky concerto, Sascha annotated my copy with some of the alternatives which had come from Leopold Auer, which he in turn had discussed with the composer.*

Everything Sascha did on the violin was utterly convincing. He had the great musical gift of communication and his playing was invariably beautifully coloured. It was an inspiration for me which has lasted half a century.

George Newman studied with Sascha Lasserson for five years from 1948. Subsequently he went into music production.

---

* See Appendix

Ruth Osborne

Both as a teenager and much later, in middle age, I had the great privilege of being Sascha's student and friend over many years.

His students were his friends, and our debt to him is enormous. He encouraged us and helped us over difficulties both musical, technical and personal. He was totally dedicated to teaching the violin and fired us with his own love of the instrument. At a glance he could see what problems we had and could show us how to solve them. "You do it like ziss," he would say in broken English, taking our instrument and demonstrating. No further words were needed!

As well as being a very great musician, he was a great human being. He had a rare integrity, modesty and unselfishness, and a delightful puckish sense of humour.

He knew his worth as a violinist but never boasted or advertised himself or curried favour with the famous, though the greatest violinists of the day recognised his qualities and treated him as their equal.

He lived simply, and seemed to have no needs other than his cigarettes. He was wonderfully good to his family, and his social life in the last years consisted entirely of going to his pupils' recitals. He never wanted anything for himself, not even a holiday. He preferred to go on practising, teaching the violin, making what was difficult appear possible because he knew how to prepare his pupils for every new leap.

It was also fascinating to hear him talk of his life at the St Petersburg Conservatoire under Auer in the company of the great violin talents of the first half of the twentieth century.

He inspired us, he nurtured us musically and we loved him, and he continues to influence us twenty years later.

Ruth Osborne, as a teenager, studied for two years in New York with Irene Zacharias (herself a pupil of Auer) prior to returning to the UK before the end of the war. She was recommended to Sascha Lasserson by Naomi Millman – Sascha's niece and also his pupil. She studied with him for a year before going to Cambridge to read English. After a gap of twenty years while bringing up her family, she recommenced lessons, studying with Sascha until his death.

Geoffrey Palmer

I first met Sascha Lasserson in 1950. Sascha was a colleague of my father, also a professional violinist. At that time I was in the Central Band of the Royal Air Force based in Uxbridge, and I wished to improve my violin playing. I regularly hitchhiked from the base to Sascha's home in Ladbroke Grove.

I clearly remember the clarity of his teaching, after a very difficult period before I came to him. The main thing, I felt, was his amazing speed in knowing the things you needed to do. His demonstrations were faultless and he had a quiet charm that I had never experienced before. I always came away from lessons with a warm feeling – very privileged to have been in the presence of a really great teacher.

I am sure he will not be forgotten by his many pupils. I think of him often with good thoughts. In fact, if it had not been for Sascha's teaching, I am sure I would not have made my playing life in the London orchestras.

Geoffrey Palmer was a pupil of Max Rostal at the Guildhall, before studying with Sascha Lasserson for three years while in the Central Band of the Royal Air Force. He then played in the Royal Opera House Orchestra, before moving to the LSO and then the RPO before returning to the ROH and subsequently the RPO again.

Tom Pilkington

I had known of Sascha Lasserson's prowess as violinist and teacher for many years from my great friend Cecil Symons, his nephew. In the 1960s, when I was a physician at St George's Hospital, Hyde Park Corner, I felt the need to improve my playing. The leader of our quartet had left and a new member decided to alternate with me as first fiddle. I asked Cecil to enquire whether Sascha would consider giving me a few lessons; he agreed and on a Thursday afternoon I trundled off to Paddington, with some trepidation.

When I got there he was taking a young boy through the Mendelssohn concerto. Sascha, as always, had his violin at the ready and demonstrated any point he wished to make. I noticed that he had a gut A string. When my time came I commented that he played on a gut A and he replied, "Well, Jascha and Mischa have gone over to gut A and I thought I would do the same." I then knew I had the great privilege to become an 'Auer grand-pupil!' He told me to get Dont Studies op.35 and Bach Solo Sonatas. He asked me to play a few scales, showed me the appropriate fingering and, when I asked him how much I should practise, he told me that he appreciated that, as a busy doctor, perhaps four hours a day would be all I could be expected to manage. I wish now I had been able or willing to do more than the odd half-hour before the weekly lessons.

At each lesson we worked on a Dont, adjusting fingering and bowing. However awful my playing, he never denigrated, always said, "Very good, but let us do it a little better!" This positive teaching technique helped not only my playing but also my medical students; I had been given proof that encouragement must always accompany correction.

Well, we plodded on with the Bach C major sonata for some

time until I plucked up enough courage to suggest that I would prefer to do something else, more relevant for my needs. Why, did I not think it great music? When I explained that I would never give a recital in the Wigmore Hall he agreed and wondered what I had in mind. A late Beethoven, I said and produced the E flat opus 127. Also great music, he exclaimed, and we dug in immediately. He became very excited since he had not played it for very many years.

Thus, my most stimulating lessons continued for 18 months. I still continue with Dont, scales and arpeggios, fingered by him, and apply his lessons now that I have retired and have time to practise one to two hours almost every day. What I now achieve in quartet playing I owe to Sascha. A truly great teacher.

Tom Pilkington is Emeritus Professor of Medicine at St George's Hospital Medical School. and a dedicated amateur violinist, who studied with Sascha Lasserson for two years while working as a consultant physician.

Carl Pini

My first lesson with Sascha Lasserson at the age of 11 was something of a shock. He immediately introduced me to C major 3rds, Schradieck and the Kreutzer Concerto No. 19. For the next six years Mr Lasserson was very much part of my life, only to be interrupted by my moving from London, subsequently spending two years on National Service. In my twenties I often asked him for help before recitals, and kept contact before leaving for Sydney.

In 1946 the main teachers in London were Albert Sammons, Max Rostal and Sascha Lasserson, and my father, the cellist Anthony Pini, felt strongly that Sascha was the best choice for me, having such a wonderful tradition and style of playing. Sascha's manner was almost unfailingly gentle, though I remember him flicking my bow off the string with impatience. Maybe his neighbours complained of incessant student noise, because the window remained shut with the gas fire blazing on the warmest days, making it difficult to concentrate after a long bus ride after school. Sascha's teaching style was not to bombard me with information, rather to demonstrate and make suggestions, particularly to practise slowly and not to copy Heifetz – he rightly suspected me of being a Heifetz freak and was against my learning the Tchaikovsky at age 15. However I prevailed for once, having learnt the first movement from memory without his knowing, even getting a date to play the whole concerto! Sascha didn't really like the Auer 'improvements' and played demonstrations with much elegance and amazing facility – a feature of his playing as I knew it.

He gave me grounding from Viotti 22, through Spohr, Vieuxtemps, Paganini and Ernst Concertos to Mendelssohn, the Bach 'studies' with Kreutzer, Dont, finally Khachaturian and Beethoven. Sascha's approach to Bach was strictly 19th century, and again his elegant style and polished phrasing were totally convincing. My own feelings about Bach and Beethoven caused some inner turmoil, but I had such respect that I tried hard to emulate his sound, especially with vibrato – he felt that English violinists used far too much, a shrewd generalisation. Compliments were few, though he did say, "Everyone has something special to offer; and you, it's the short, sharp trill" in Tartini-Kreisler Variations! Also, memorably, "Keep your stiff loose."

There was never any doubt that his teaching was the real thing and I always left his room or studio with a greater appreciation of the work I was studying. Sascha's great gift of imparting the best traditions of violin playing was indefinable, and it's a privilege to look back and be grateful for his profound influence.

Carl Pini began studying with Sascha Lasserson at the age of 11 and continued for six years. He led the London String Quartet before moving to Sydney, where he formed the Sinfonia of Sydney and the Carl Pini Quartet. He returned to London as Leader of the Philharmonia, subsequently returning to Australia as leader of the Melbourne Symphony Orchestra, and later as Principal in the Sydney Symphony Orchestra. He continues to lead the Quartet.

Felix Pooler

I was keeping an appointment at 60 Ladbroke Grove for my first violin lesson with Mr Lasserson at 11 am one Tuesday morning in September 1959. I could see an elderly gentleman coming towards me carrying a shaped fiddle case and we met each other at the door. "Are you the person coming about violin lessons?" he asked. "Yes," I replied, and he unlocked the door, led the way upstairs to a frugally furnished room, drew up two chairs, motioning me to sit down, then sat down himself and just turned and looked at me. After some hesitation, I told him I was worried about my playing, needed help, and Graham Riddell, one of his pupils, had recommended that I come to him.

He asked me which pieces I had studied and I mentioned some, but when I came to theWieniawski Concerto in D minor he asked, "Have you done plenty of preparatory exercises in thirds, sixths and octaves?" I had to say that I hadn't. He said, somewhat wistfully, "Poor you!"

From his whole bearing, I had respected him from the first moment that I met him at the door, and every encounter with him confirmed that over the next two or three years that I came for lessons. He was a superb teacher and in this first lesson he made me do the scale of G major four octaves and the arpeggio, to be practised every day in the future, and he wrote out for me exercises in thirds, double-stopped arpeggios, and some indications how to practise Dont Study No.1 (see Appendix).

His own playing was perfect, with a very big repertoire, and so much from memory; on one occasion he played to me the whole of Paganini's *Moto Perpetuo* from memory and, reaching the end, he just leaned against the piano and breathed in deeply! Very down-to-earth, and nothing of the pompous old man about him in the slightest.

He certainly could handle young people, and on one occasion I saw him teaching a young Indian aged 12 years, using a violin made by his father (Mr Lasserson told me), and, in the course of his lesson on Sarasate Variations, the boy did something wrong and Mr Lasserson told him quite good-naturedly, "I told you not to do that," and pressed his left hand up to the ribs of the violin when playing in the third position. The boy was quite happy with that treatment and the father, who was present, smiled, looking on.

How different my future might have been if at, say, twelve years of age, I could have had my very first encounter with Mr Lasserson. It was a privilege to have met him.

Felix Pooler studied at the Manchester RCM before further studies with Sascha Lasserson. He was in the Covent Garden Orchestra for ten years before moving to the Liverpoool Philharmonic. He taught violin for Staffordshire County Council for twenty years until 1997 when – "quite happily" – he became redundant.

Daphne Pritchard
a Parent's view

My son Jonathan had his first proper violin lesson in early May 1972, when he was ten. Six months later Dennis Bayer (our Church organist), heard him play. Dennis was the secretary of the Martin Music Scholarship Fund; he knew Geoffrey Trabichoff and, the day after hearing Jonathan, took him to play to Geoff, who asked to hear him again in a year. Jonathan played to him again when he was nearly twelve, and lessons began with Geoff at once. Eight months later Geoff was off to Portugal as leader of the Gulbenkian Orchestra. Jonathan was very sad about this, but Geoff very kindly asked if he could take him to play to Sascha Lasserson; he explained that Sascha did not teach children, but nevertheless he wanted Sascha to hear Jonathan. I had often heard Geoff talk about Sascha with such awe and affection, and so was very thrilled that I was actually going with Jonathan to meet him.

At the end of October 1974, when Jonathan was twelve, we arrived at Sascha's studio in Shepherd's Bush. This dear elderly gentleman, still with his very strong Russian accent, came to greet us. He was so small in stature, yet bigger in himself than anyone I have ever met. The memories of that afternoon will always live with me, and his words "I would like to teach Jonathan" were magic!

To my utter amazement, two weeks later – on November 9th – Jonathan and I were travelling from Thorpe Bay in Essex to London, a journey we were to repeat almost every Saturday for many years. No school holidays! Only if a Saturday fell too near to Christmas, or for family holidays, did we miss a lesson. Sascha became part of our lives. It was suggested that, because of Sascha's accent, I should buy a note book and attend each lesson, taking notes in case Jonathan did not understand any point. However, Jonathan could always understand; I kept very quiet about this because it was so wonderful and such a privilege to listen to Sascha and watch him teach. In all the years he taught Jonathan I never once heard him raise his voice. He taught with such understanding and encouragement and enthusiasm, in such a patient, gentle, and loving way. He never once spoke down to Jonathan. He had a wonderful way of talking to him, and taught him as if Jonathan was his friend. Jonathan never once said that he did not want to go for his lesson, or was worried or anxious - which might easily have been the case, having lessons from so great a teacher. To quote from a conversation I had with a professional violinist, on hearing the results of Jonathan's audition, "Mr Lasserson is one of the best violin teachers in the country – in fact, I can say beyond doubt, the greatest."

By June the following year, 1975, I felt I could ask Sascha if he would let me take a photograph of him with Jonathan. I had been longing to ask him, and he seemed really happy about it. Out he trotted, an 85-year old with his 13-year old student, both with their violins and bows. This photograph has been on our mantelpiece for 28 years. On the back I have written a few details; one was that Jonathan was 4ft.11ins – just about the same height as his beloved teacher!

It was at this time that Jonathan was studying the Bach Double, which was probably the most moving of all the music I sat through. Because Sascha was always playing to Jonathan, to show him exactly how he wanted him to play and was only satisfied when he interpreted the music as did Sascha himself, the final result was that it just sounded 'as one'. I could have wept with overwhelming emotion every time. From his comments, Sascha enjoyed this to the full, and so did Jonathan! Sascha always commented about their amazing age difference, and then he and Jonathan would look at each other, both beaming from ear to ear. Sascha looked as if he was a teenager too! Such joy for me to be there; what richness Sascha brought to my life as well as my son's, and how I wished that my own violin-playing had been good enough to play with him too.

After a while, Sascha found that the journey to his Shepherd's

Bush studio was getting too much for him. My heart sank. I thought he was going to give up teaching. But no. He asked if I would mind bringing Jonathan to his house each week, saying that he was sorry that it would take us so much longer. By now, this dear man had become not just part of our lives but had worked his way into our hearts, and Jonathan would have been devastated if Sascha had decided not to teach him any more. From then on, Sascha telephoned me every Saturday after breakfast to tell me that all was well with him and to find out if we could make our usual visit. Of course! Each week I looked forward to his call. By then I sat, notebook in hand still, as Sacha worked on this or that concerto. It was becoming more emotional than ever, listening to this genius play, passing on his gift to a young teenager. As the years passed – he had been teaching Jonathan for over three years by this time – Sascha began to tire more easily, yet still seemed to get great joy from his amazing gift of teaching. I felt I wanted to hold back every single day, to stop time in its tracks, feeling so aware that he could not live forever.

Sometimes, he would phone to say that he had not been too well so would we leave the lesson until next week. I worried about him until I had his call the next weekend. Often he was feeling better, so another lesson was arranged. These lessons became more treasured, not only for Jonathan but also for me. Inevitably, the time came when the telephone did not ring

I cannot remember who telephoned me to say that Sascha had died; I suppose it was his son. All I know is that I sobbed and sobbed, more so than when my own much-loved grandfather died. Sascha had so enriched the world of music and had given Jonathan part of himself, an unbelievably precious gift which he had given so generously to so many violinists. Over the years Jonathan and I had grown to love this dear, dear man. Having sat, enthralled, through so many hours of his teaching, I think the best way I can describe his gift is to say, "Sascha Lasserson taught with love."

Jonathan Pritchard

I began playing the violin at the age of 9 at school, not long after I had gone through an operation to restore my hearing, as I had been going deaf from a very early age. When I think back to how I first met Sascha, I am still stunned, and can only believe that it was fate which played a major role at this fantastic time in my life.

After my first teachers, I was lucky enough to study with Geoffrey Trabichoff after winning a Martin Music Scholarship. I was nearly 12, and had so much to learn. During my lessons with Geoffrey, he spoke of his teacher Sascha Lasserson, and I was delighted to have an opportunity to meet Sascha after I had been with Geoffrey for 8 months. Geoffrey had told my mother and me that he did not think it would be possible to have lessons with Sascha, because he just taught people who needed to polish their playing and technique before concerts. I was, therefore, very pleased to have an opportunity just to play to this great man.

I remember when we arrived in Shepherd's Bush for the first time; it was a cold October day, and the whole experience was one that I have never forgotten. I can start by saying that it was not what I had expected! I was small for my age and, when I met Sascha, he was not much taller than me. During the time I played for Sascha he smoked continuously and I remember thinking – how has this man managed to get so old and still be living! Of course, at my age of 13, Sascha appeared to be at least 150! However, as soon as he picked up his violin and began to play, I understood that it did not matter if he had been 300 years old. I cannot put into words this experience. It was not only what I heard coming out of his violin, but also the way it made me feel. Of all the things I have gone through in my life, this one moment taught me that greatness is so much more than what we can see and hear

At the end of that amazing afternoon, he told my mother that he would like to teach me. I do not think that I really understood, at the age of 13, what that meant, but today I think I must have been one of the luckiest children on the planet. When I look back to the four years I had with Sascha, I could almost weep. He was such a kind man, and never once did he make me feel as if he was the master and I was to do everything he said (although that was what I nearly always did in the end). He never raised his voice; he simply showed me what he meant by playing to me. I did not always enjoy what he asked me to play, and all the people who ever studied with him will know what I mean when I say that he was very keen on scales and studies! However, this was always matched by his enthusiastic teaching of Vivaldi, Bach, Beethoven, Brahms, Fritz Kreisler - the list goes on and on. The piece I will never forget studying with him is the Bach Double. The memory of playing this, with Sascha at my side, and the music we made, will stay with me until the day I die. I know that, for my mother, it was one of the greatest and most special moments of all my lessons. She always came to the lessons with me, for she told me that I might have problems understanding Sascha's very strong Russian accent. I think she was mainly there because both of us loved this wonderful old man..

The last two works I studied with him were the Mendelssohn and Bruch G-minor concertos. I knew, at this time, that he would not live much longer. Each week, my mother would wait for a phone-call to say we could come and so we would make the trip to his home; he had stopped teaching at the Shepherd's Bush studio because it was too much for him. He would sit and play to me as though it was only the love of music that was keeping him alive.

It is both wonderful and painful for me to look back at my time with Sascha. It is wonderful because nobody who met this man could ever doubt that, to be in the same room and hear him play, brought me joy, richness, love of music, and so much more than I could ever put into words. His way of teaching was, and still is to my mind, the best that the world has had to offer.

It is painful because Sascha took with him to the grave so much that he did not have time to pass on to me.

When you have had a teacher like Sascha Lasserson, it is impossible to replace him with anyone else. I did, however, continue to play and study with other teachers, and went on to play as a professional. Later , I moved to New Zealand; there, I had the honour of performing a double concerto for violin and cello in Wellington, written for myself and my first wife by Dorothy Buchanan.

Today, I do not play professionally any more. Perhaps, if I had had more time with Sascha and had worked harder, things would be different. But that does not detract from the experience of spending so much time, as a young boy, in the same room as a genius. It was a privilege and an honour to have known him.

In conclusion, I recall some words he once uttered to me, "If you do not practice for one day, you will notice. If you do not practice for two days, your teacher will notice. And, if you do not practice for three days, the audience will notice!"

Jonathan Pritchard began his studies, as a boy, with Geoffrey Trabichoff. He went on to study with Sascha Lasserson from the age of 12 until Sascha's death four years later. He moved to work in New Zealand. He left the profession after many years, and now lives and works in Stockholm.

Edmund Reid

I will never forget the first time I met Sascha Lasserson. Having been awarded a full-time scholarship by the Jamaican Government, and on the strong recommendation of David McCallum (former leader of the RPO under Beecham) and other distinguished players, I was auditioning for Sascha to see if he would take me on as a pupil.

I played the Bruch G minor. Then I was slightly taken aback when he asked me to play some scales. I seem to remember G major four octaves (not just three), and some four-octave arpeggios; and of course his beloved (I was to find out later) thirds. After I had finished the audition, he took a long look at me and said, "You have good fingers ... Now we work!"

And work I did. For six weeks I was put on a regime of scales of all sorts, especially on one string from one end of the fingerboard to the other, with all possible combinations of fingers. Lots of thirds of course. At the end of this intensive period, he took another long look at me and with that almost beatific smile of his said, "You have worked well ... Now we play!"

So it was straight into the Vieuxtemps 5th Concerto and the Dont Studies (the first one in chords Sascha cleverly adapted as a bowing exercise as well). Then all of the Paganini Caprices.

Speaking of Vieuxtemps 5, there is a very difficult run at the end of the cadenza, which I had to have ready at all times. In the three years I was with Sascha as a full-time student, he would often take me by surprise by requesting a performance of this famous run. He used to say that there were certain passages in the literature that you have to "have in your pocket". The two very difficult triplet passages in the first movement of the Mendelssohn Concerto were among his other examples; also the last page of *Rondo Capriccioso*.

He himself had the whole repertoire 'in his pocket'. Although I was brought up in Jamaica on records of Heifetz and Milstein, and had heard all the great players in concert tours to my country, I was awe-struck by Sascha's playing in the studio. He would throw off peerlessly, and fearlessly, the fiendishly difficult Ernst *Last Rose of Summer* variations, then move you almost to tears with his beautiful, sensitive playing of a Bach Solo Sonata movement. His playing of Paganini Caprices, as with everything else, was clean and effortless. The only worry I ever had listening to Sascha in the studio was whether the ever-growing ash on his ever-present cigarette would fall on his jacket lapel or his fiddle!

Sascha was very much against the rough and ready style of playing and what he called 'short cuts'. On the other hand, he always built on the talents of his pupils. None of the "We must start from scratch and play my way" which many ego-driven teachers insist on, no matter how good the pupil was to start with.

What he did insist on was absolute accuracy of intonation, clarity of fingerwork and beauty of tone. In order to achieve these criteria, he above all taught me how to practise; to use not just my fingers, but also my brain.

Edmund Reid came to England on a Jamaican Government Scholarship at the age of 16, to study with Sascha Lasserson. He remained with Sascha, full-time, for three years before joining the London freelance world. Subsequently he became Co-leader of Welsh National Opera Orchestra, then Principal at the Royal Opera House. He was for many years been Co-leader of the English National Opera Orchestra. In 1985 he formed the sonata team, The Virtuoso Duo, with his wife, the pianist Gretta Barrow.

Graham Riddell

I had just finished at the Royal Manchester College of Music after three years, having been a pupil of Thomas Matthews and Clifford Knowles, and had come to London. My wish was to carry on with my violin studies and, through a colleague, I was introduced to one of the viola players from the BBC Concert Orchestra. He had studied with Mr Lasserson and suggested that I try to become one of Mr Lasserson's pupils, and so this was how I began my many years of study with one of the truly great teachers.

I am sometimes asked – What was Mr Lasserson like? Firstly, as a man – he was of slight build, always well dressed. Even in the hot weather he would dress correctly, and his manner was quiet, rather softly spoken and unassuming at all times. Secondly, as a violinist – the moment he put the violin to his chin, put the bow on the string, one knew that here was a great virtuoso. While he played there was barely any movement save that of his fingers and bow; his fingers remained very close to the strings. It appeared as though he played with his eyes closed, but this was not so; he was watching his fingers all the time and how they were placed on the fingerboard.

Whilst I was at Manchester I had gone through some of the repertoire, including some unaccompanied Bach, so perhaps I knew a little. After I had been with Sascha a while, we started work on the Bach Solo Sonatas. He opened the book at the beginning and so we commenced the G minor. Two years later we had completed all six, after which he opened the book at the beginning, and we started all over again; this time it only took 18 months. Then I was expected to be in a position to work at them, and he would ask me to play any of his choice, always stressing the point that they were for a lifetime's study, and this I have always tried to bear in mind.

As a teacher, he encouraged his pupils; even though one might have great difficulty doing what he wanted, he was never in the slightest discouraging – and this helped to forge the bond between master and pupil. He was always ready to give credit to other players and teachers for – in Sascha's case – there was not just his way to play the violin. Other teachers might insist on this, but Sascha was above that kind of thing.

On one occasion he kindly invited me to his home (not for a lesson), and he played for me, a complete recital, and I called out the things I wished him to play. Naturally, he didn't know what I was going to request, so there was no question of him having prepared anything beforehand; yet, at the drop of a hat, he was able to play these things, as a finished performance. On one occasion he said to me, "One should be able to pick up the violin at any moment and be able to play," and on the occasion which I have mentioned, he certainly proved his point.

His death, the passing of a great teacher and great friend, was a great blow to all his pupils. Above my piano hangs a photograph of Sascha Lasserson, inscribed to me. So often, when I practise, I think of him and wish he were with me to help with my problems. He is always so very near to me.

It is said that there is no greater love than that of a pupil for his master.

Graham Riddell studied with Clifford Knowles and Thomas Matthews at the Royal Manchester College of Music. Then he joined the Orchestra of the Royal Horse Guards. During this time he studied with Sascha Lasserson for twelve years. He has been a violin teacher since his return to civilian life.

Tessa Robbins

Over the years I had valuable training from several first class professors and when I sought Mr. Lasserson's help I was well launched on my solo career. My last teacher had introduced physical attitudes which were foreign to me, and although I had largely managed on my own to regain my former freedom, there was one vital respect in which I had great difficulty. I was very anxious about this, and friends recommended that I should ask Sascha Lasserson for advice.

After I had played my party piece and a scale at his request he asked me, "Why have you come?" I replied, "I don't know how to hold the violin!". "That's easy," was his answer and he showed me in four simple moves. Just one week later my reflection in the mirror reminded me of the photograph of myself as a five-year-old violinist; the comfortable stance was exactly the same. The information, presented with total simplicity, drew me in gratitude for ever to this master teacher.

[The beauty of the method referred to above is that it adapts to the physique of the player and to the model of instrument, chin and shoulder rest.

1 Take the violin and place the button centrally against the throat.

2 Move the left hand to support the neck and with the right hand angle the instrument leftward until its back comes in contact with the collarbone.

There is now a large space between instrument and shoulder.

3 Still holding the violin in position 2 with the right hand, drop the left hand down to the side then throw the whole arm up from the back muscles and support the violin lightly at the neck.

The space between shoulder and violin is reduced and you can now see how large a shoulder pad is needed.

4 Lastly drop the weight of the head with the side of the jaw resting on a well designed and suitably positioned chinrest.]

It is said that Auer taught mainly by illustration, playing a great deal in class, and similarly Sascha had such a power of diagnosis and the ability to communicate remedy without complication. Certainly he never again needed to refer to my technical problem, for it had been solved in half a minute and there were more important aspects of music and interpretation to discuss in succeeding lessons.

He was completely unpretentious, never finding it necessary to impress people. His thoughts were all for his students, whom he loved as he loved his family. With his warmth of personality he also had an impish sense of humour, chuckling in disarming delight at our stunned admiration of his awesome technical brilliance when illustrating a point in a lesson. But ultimately it is not firstly with admiration that one remembers Sascha, nor even of gratitude towards him, but more of thanksgiving that one was fortunate to draw close to this dear human being.

Tessa Robbins studied with Isolde Menges (herself a pupil of Auer) and with Albert Sammons at the Royal College of Music. She was soloist at Henry Wood Promenade concerts, finalist at the Queen Elizabeth Competion in Brussels (1955) and winner of the Munich International Violin Competition (1956). After this she sought advice from Sascha Lasserson and studied with him for a further three years, inspired by his humanity and wisdom.

Jack Rothstein

I came to this country in 1946 after having played in an ENSA dance band for three years. My violin tuition had started late, at the age of nine, and had been of very low quality. My violin playing was based on enthusiasm and, I suppose, talent. I was very anxious to establish who could guide me to a better understanding of violin technique and enquired of all the violinists that I met who was the best teacher in London. The unanimous answer was Sascha Lasserson.

I came to him as a very unconventional pupil. I had a gipsy orchestra in a night club called 'The Society' in Jermyn Street and often performed live on television from Alexandra Palace. I relied on a good memory as I really did not even read music that well. My bow arm was not comfortable and I was quite surprised not to start my lessons on open strings. In retrospect I think that Mr Lasserson was very concerned that my confidence should be maintained and boosted. During the year I spent with him he made me play the concertos of Mendelssohn, Tchaikovsky, Lalo Symphonie Espagnol, etc. He was always very encouraging.

I was always amazed at his own meticulous technique. He could demonstrate anything. Even more notable was his genuine kindness.

Two stories that stick in my mind are of the occasion of David Oistrakh's first concert in London. Mr Lasserson (who was considerably older), when asked "What do you think of him?" commented "A talented boy!" He also said of Heifetz, most affectionately, "I heard him play the Mendelssohn concerto in Russia when he was eight years old, and he hasn't improved!"

The last time I saw Mr Lasserson was at recording sessions where Heifetz was playing the Scottish Fantasie by Max Bruch. I was playing in the orchestra, and Mr Lasserson had come to listen. It was on this day that I realised he was one of the very few people in the world who was allowed to address the great violinist as Jascha, and not the formal Mr Heifetz.

Jack Rothstein entered the profession as a dance-band musician, working with ENSA, before running his own band. In 1948, he came to study with Sascha Lasserson for a year, subsequently becoming a freelance orchestral player and soloist.

Alla Sharova

I was introduced to Mr Lasserson by Brian Underwood shortly after my arrival from Leningrad (St Petersburg), where I studied the violin, first at the specialist music school and later at the Conservatoire. From an early age we all knew the names of Leopold Auer and his illustrious pupils, as there still remained quite a few of our teachers who themselves had studied either with Auer or his assistants. During my years at the Conservatoire, I received violin lessons in the Leopold Auer room, where hung a large painting of a rather stern-looking Auer watching my every move. The thrill of meeting Sascha Lasserson for the first time was rather like experiencing the rebirth of what was, for us in Russia, a legendary period in the history of violin playing. Alexander Lvovich – as I called him – was an extremely kind, considerate and thoughtful pedagogue, a wonderful musician and an astonishing violinist, who retained his infectious enthusiasm for the violin, his sense of humour, and his incredible strength of spirit to the end of his life.

Once, when I asked him how he was, he said, "Oh, I have pains in my shoulders – rheumatism. And I tell you, doctors cannot help. I, myself, found what to do: if I practise the Chaconne for an hour – the pain goes!" He was extraordinarily sensitive. On one occasion, feeling I was upset by something, he conducted the lesson, as usual, in his beautiful Russian, breaking off occasionally to relate an amusing anecdote. At the end, when I was leaving, he said in English, looking at me with his gentle smile, "Keep cheering up!"

On another occasion I complained of a particularly bad violinist I had to share a desk with. "Awful bow-arm, dreadful fingering, no sense of style, ghastly vibrato," I moaned. Alexander Lvovich listened quietly, then winked at me and said, "Well, if there were no bad violinists, how would you know who were the good ones? See, even bad violinists can be useful!" This innocent joke, I realised later, contained a veiled lesson on tolerance.

I found Lasserson always encouraging and very supportive. When I was asked to play the Tchaikovsky Concerto at St John's Smith Square for the first time with orchestra, I was extremely apprehensive, but Lasserson said quite firmly, "Oh, what nonsense – of course you can play it beautifully!" I had played the concerto as a student and knew it very well, but Lasserson's lessons opened up quite a different approach for me – much more imaginative and relaxed. He patiently 'nursed' me through all the preparation for my big day, came to my rehearsal with the orchestra and was quite upset when I was not able to borrow a good violin. From that occasion onwards, Lasserson guided me through all my performances of the Mendelssohn and Sibelius concertos, Beethoven, Debussy, Prokofiev and many other sonatas. His teaching of unaccompanied Bach was superb and his demonstrations – of the Chaconne and the Fugues in particular – absolutely unforgettable. Every lesson with him was anticipated eagerly – like a special occasion.

I have always loved teaching. For students of the St Petersburg Conservatoire this was a compulsory discipline for the entire duration of the course (5 years). Our tutor in this subject was Yakov Ryabinkov, a concert violinist and excellent teacher, who had studied with Auer's pupil, Lubov Segal. We had individual lessons twice a week with a child-beginner, once in the presence of a tutor and once without; thus we were checked and corrected every week. Every June we had an exam at which we presented our pupils to a panel of senior professors with a programme of scales, studies, concerto movement and a short piece. We were also subjected to a viva voce in pedagogy. Finally, on graduation, the teaching qualification was included in our diploma.

So, when I began teaching at the Royal Academy of Music in London, I felt quite confident. Among my first pupils was a very intelligent girl who, like others, lacked foundation. I started building her up with great zest and enthusiasm: scales, Sevcik,

Schradieck, studies, study-concertos, etc. – the sort of work we had to do in Russia. The girl was improving rapidly, but suddenly – a stumbling block: spiccato. She was doing the Wieniawski Concerto No.2 but, in spite of all the exercises and demonstrations I gave her, simply could not make the bow bounce. Feeling quite desperate, I confided my sorrows ("teaching failure," I said) to Lasserson. He advised me to bring the girl to him for a lesson. On that memorable day Lasserson spent a lot of time talking to Sophie about everything under the sun – except spiccato. Then he said, "All right, Sophie, let us hear the 1st and 2nd movements of the concerto with the piano." Halfway through, my pupil visibly relaxed and began to play really well. Lasserson praised her to the skies and then said, "Carry on, Sophie." My heart sank as she started the last movement, but to my sheer amazement she played it brilliantly without any problem with spiccato at all. I was stunned when, at the end, Lasserson exclaimed, "Well done, Sophie, wonderful spiccato!"

This was a most valuable lesson in psychology. The following week I had an explanation. "The girl is very tense anyway, you made it worse by continuously working on the stroke – after a while one should relax a pupil and take the mind away from the problem." I have never forgotten this lesson and have always implemented Lasserson's principles in my teaching.

I was lucky to be introduced by Alexander Lvovich to Nathan Milstein – one of my violinistic idols, who became my inspiration and my mentor for quite a few years. I enjoyed going to Milstein's home in Belgravia for lessons, which often were followed by tea, chats and watching the 'movies' with him and his wife, Thérèse. Milstein, a superb violinist and a great artist, had a very deep respect for Lasserson; he would often say to me, "I am not a teacher, Lasserson is a real pedagogue – a great teacher!"

I could have written a book about Sascha Lasserson – he lives vividly in my memory and his influence on me still remains strong. But what made him really very special was his genuine human qualities. He was an absolute gentleman and a very humble person. Nowadays when people are busy promoting and projecting themselves, when anybody and everybody gives master-classes, when the violin is sometimes just a working tool, when there are hype and marketing images instead of musicianship, the unforgettable example of Sascha Lasserson as a wonderful violin-ist, a great and dedicated teacher, superb musician and a warm-hearted, compassionate and modest human being is like a magical torch pointing the right way, for all who had the privilege of knowing and studying with him.

Alla Sharova studied at the Leningrad Specialist Music School, where she was a Gold Medallist, and graduated from the Conservatoire with distinc-tion. On coming to the West, she studied with Rostislav Dubinsky (the founder and leader of the Borodin Quartet) before going on to study with Sascha Lasserson and subsequently with Nathan Milstein. She has free-lanced as a concerto-soloist and recitalist all over Europe as well as perform-ing in India, Australia and New Zealand. In 1979, she premiered Schnittke's Suite in the Old Style at the Wigmore Hall, and the British composers John Mayer and Andrew Downie have written works specially for her – Mayer's Jatiswaram in 1996, and Downie's God Marduk in 1999.

She has led the Nevsky Quartet, and has worked with the actress Mary Chater in presenting programmes of Music and Poetry. As a dedicated teacher, she has been on the staff of the Royal Academy, as well as teaching students from Oxford, Cambridge and City Universities, adjudicating at music festivals and coaching at summer schools.

Ursula Snow

I have been asked, as a former pupil of Sascha Lasserson, to write down what I remember about the man, and his teaching. Over the years I have, of course, met a number of violinists who were also pupils of his, at one time or another, and I have been impressed by the variety of ways in which so many have been influenced, helped, encouraged, and strengthened by their contact with this remarkable man. Most have had more experience of different teachers than I, with the result that they have been more able to make more comparisons than I can. I came to him several years after leaving the RCM, where I had achieved more musically than technically – and was very much aware of this disadvantage. I was trying to make my way in a competitive and demanding profession while having little faith in my technical equipment. In spite of long hours of hard work, I seldom felt secure in performance, and thus seldom enjoyed playing in public. So, having been advised by several excellent players who had been helped by Sascha to approach him, I eventually plucked up courage and did so – a decision which I have never regretted.

It was in a limbo of despair that I went for my first lesson. I expected to have a tough time, but was past caring as long as he was willing to help me and as long as I could make some improvement. What I hadn't expected was the warmth, kindness and encouragement with which I was received. He was strict and demanding, but never discouraging. Looking back, it seems to me that one of the most important qualities of his teaching was just his ability to relate to each pupil as an individual – with each one's specific weaknesses (and possibly strengths) – in order to give the specific help and advice needed. Lessons were purposeful, but unhurried. I enjoyed his brilliant demonstration – often on my own instrument – and learnt a great deal by watching and listening. His patient encouragement helped me to overcome difficulties and reduce stress – I clearly remember the look of amusement on his face at the huge amount of inappropriate effort I might be making over what should have been a comparatively simple action, and the way he would, with perhaps only a wink and no word spoken, get me to relax so that a perceived technical difficulty suddenly ceased to be a problem.

I think the characteristic element of his style of teaching which most impressed me was its apparent simplicity with a touch of sheer common sense, and I have tried to apply these qualities to my own teaching and playing. He spoke little in my lessons – usually preferring to demonstrate – and was constantly vigilant, alert, perceptive and positive. He enabled me to tackle music which I would have rejected because of its sheer difficulty, and encouraged me in such a way that I felt able to teach myself – and with confidence. When I consider how spasmodic my lessons were, and over such a comparatively short period, the improvement he helped me achieve was spectacular. Never having been very interested in technical brilliance for its own sake, my need to interpret and express musical ideas was always, until then, severely hampered by a lack of technical equipment – mostly as a result of poor grounding – very frequently found in this country at that time.

Sascha Lasserson, in his quiet way, has had an important impact on the art of teaching and playing the violin. Countless violinists will always remember him with affection and gratitude for the influence he had on their development as players, and for the warm concern he showed for his pupils – long after they had left. Like me they will be, consciously or unconsciously, passing some of his influence on to their own pupils. Many will remember his fascinating and often amusing anecdotes about some of the great violinists he knew so well. However, one of my 'favourites' has always been the one about the window cleaner who, while cleaning the windows in Sascha's flat when Sascha was doing some slow scale practice, eventually couldn't resist asking Sascha (at that time about 65 years old) how long he had been playing the violin. "About 60 years," came the reply. Window cleaner (astonished) – "I should've thought you'd 'ave been a bit better by now!"

Ursula Snow is a freelance violinist and teacher. She studied first with Isolde Menges and – after years in the profession – went to Sascha Lasserson. She now works also as a chamber music player with the Westbourne Concordia group.

Pamela Spofforth

For me, the lasting impression of one's studies with Sascha Lasserson in the '50s (and '60s when I was invited to take pupils to play to him) was that the music was always paramount whilst, of course, technique was essential.

Sascha's ability to put his finger on the cause of any problem and to offer as many solutions as were necessary, was remarkable. His demonstrations on his beloved Spiritus Sorsana were illuminating, and he expected one to be sufficient, although he never showed impatience if it were not. Very generous with his lesson time, his stamina, even in his late seventies, was amazing.

The music of Bach, of course, was dear to him – he loved my Pressenda violin and often took it to play the Chaconne – having just lit a cigarette. I watched anxiously as the ash grew in length, perilously close to the precious varnish!

Sometimes in a playful mood, whilst getting out one's instrument at the beginning of a lesson, Sascha would say, "Do you know who this is? ... And this?" and would proceed to play extracts from half a dozen concertos in the manner and imitating the tone of as many well-known soloists – his face creasing into a mischievous grin as one recognised the 'victims'.

Since studying with Lasserson I have come to appreciate more and more that his concept of musical styles went far deeper and wider than that of many of his contemporaries. His Mozart had grace; his Brahms the advantage of nearness to the composer and to Joachim. He imparted the importance of the particular and characteristic tone quality, length of quaver and tempi, and subtleties of shifting (in the Franck Sonata for instance, so often overlooked today with 'better' fingering in one position). His interpretation of the Tchaikovsky Concerto avoided sentimentality in the Canzonetta. Excessive vibrato was anathema to him – and, of course, the slightest lapse of intonation caused a look of pained surprise!

Always willing to give help in programme building and to hear a recital before the event and to give advice and encouragement, his friendship was invaluable. The only shadow of doubt I ever felt was his apparent fear of memorising. Fortunately, this did not afflict me personally, but it puzzled me.

Sascha Lasserson was, without doubt, one of the greatest teachers of the century in the great Auer tradition: he was proud to quote specific concepts, without the restrictions of 'a method'. Scales, yes; any scale at any time and not necessarily starting on the tonic! He thought 4ths important and often neglected. Relaxation was essential and extraneous movement to be avoided – the sound was what mattered.

In the interview with Mavis Bacca, printed in The Strad. July 1956 (a copy of which I have, signed by Sascha Lasserson), he was asked what he thought of British violin students.

"There is," he declared, "no dearth of talent in England. The difficulty lies, not in bringing out the latent gift, but in the system of education which blasts many a promising career before it has had time to mature. School, with its manifold exigencies, cuts across the embryo artist as surely as a scythe across growing grass."

The system of priority for academic work and exams at fifteen and seventeen without sufficient time for practice, to develop technique and acquiring the repertoire, followed by three or four years at a college, leaves little option for the student. Then "the obligation of earning a living (and) the aspiring musician turns to orchestral work as the surest form of income. Practice becomes sporadic and of secondary consideration ..."

Sascha Lasserson was an advocate of the class method of teaching employed abroad, and regretted that lack of time prevents its development in England. I was shown the photograph in his room of Auer's class, with Elman, Heifetz, Burgin, Zimbalist, Pirastro and himself as a boy, which obviously evoked treasured memories for him. What a pity the video was not invented then.

Pamela Spofforth was co-founder, with Elizabeth Hewlins, of Pro-Corda (National School for Young Chamber Music Players) and taught at the Junior RCM. She studied with Eda Kersey for three years then became a pupil of Sascha Lasserson, with whom she studied for ten years.

Geoffrey Trabichoff

Sascha Lasserson was wonderful. He was a wonderful teacher and, even at the age of 78, which is when I first got to know him, a wonderful violinist. His undogmatic approach to violin playing, and especially to fingerings and bowings was hugely refreshing after six years at one of London's music colleges with a teacher who insisted on the slavish copying of his every violinistic whim. Sascha encouraged one to think for oneself; surely what teaching is all about. He was always ready to discuss fingerings and bowings and to give reasons for his preferences, but he never insisted on change just to match some preconceived idea of his own. Practical as he was, he might occasionally comment, "You're playing that just fine, but your bowing/fingering is pretty unconventional and you should know that most people would find this easier," with the wisdom of an experienced and committed teacher. Such a modus operandi was liberating and confidence-inspiring.

Two illustrations of this that stand out in my memory: after a couple of months as a pupil of Sascha's, I was to play the Schubert G minor Sonatina at some small recital. I put the music on the stand at the start of my lesson and the conversation went like this: Sascha, peering over the top of his wire-rim glasses at the music: "What's this?" Trabichoff: "It's the Schubert G minor Sonatina, I have to play it next week." Sascha: "Well go and play it! You're a musical chap, you'll do a very nice job, enjoy yourself." On another occasion I had played him Elgar's *La Capriceuse* and, after working on the 'flying staccato' in the outer sections of this piece, Sascha closed the music without any discussion of the middle section's big G string tune. I opened the music again and asked: "What about the middle section?" Sascha: "Funny thing, you play that totally differently to me, where I would slow down a bit you push on, where I would do a crescendo, you play a diminuendo;

but it was beautiful, full of conviction, don't change a thing." This egalitarian approach was noticed by my accompanist too, who commented after a lesson on the Mendelssohn concerto, that it was very rare to see a pupil and teacher doing obviously different bowings in certain passages. She played for a lot of violin students at one of the London colleges and said that the violin teachers there would have insisted on conformity.

As all of the above makes abundantly clear, Sascha was a born teacher. He was a professional. I was sometimes present when he auditioned prospective pupils and once or twice expressed my surprise at his having accepted someone whom I would have considered below the level of talent that would have engaged his interest. But Sascha might say, "Not a big talent, I agree, but he has good hands; I'll be able to help him up a couple of rungs on the ladder."

My own first lesson was a revelation. I walked in unable to play a D major scale in 3 octaves and walked out able to rattle off a G major scale in 4 octaves. It was like magic! He could also teach 'up-bow staccato' which, according to Flesch, is unteachable. Sascha's hands-on approach gave me a very serviceable staccato which I never possessed before and I have successfully employed his method with students of my own.

Sascha would always enquire of a new student what make of bow they used. If the answer was "Sartory," he would immediately respond with, "I bet mine is longer than yours!" and the startled pupil would suddenly find his bow being measured against his teacher's and falling short, as it were. Sascha always enjoyed pulling this trick and had, in fact, never found another Sartory the equal of his!

Sascha had a great sense of humour. As an 80-year-old he went to his doctor for a repeat prescription of pills which helped his rheumatism. He found a locum in situ who insisted on his stripping to the waist for an examination that consisted mainly of prodding. "Well, Mr Lasserson," said the enthusiastic youngster, still prodding, "we can't give you new bones, you know." "In that case," retorted Sascha, "would you mind leaving the old ones intact!" Violinistically, his sense of humour could be mischievously insouciant; "Violin playing's easy," he would say. "Just make a beautiful sound, play in tune and phrase nicely." On the other hand, "The complexity of violin playing is such that you need to be talented just in order to play badly!" was a favourite of Sascha's. He could also be very funny, though unintentionally so, if ever he had anything critical to say about Mischa Elman, Jascha Heifetz or Nathan Milstein, all pupils of Leopold Auer, as was he. He would first peer right around the room for non-existent eavesdroppers and then make his critique in a sort of strangulated stage whisper, seeming shocked at his own audacity.

That Sascha Lasserson was held in high esteem by his colleagues is evidenced by the fact that Milstein, then living in London, would occasionally send a taxi for him so that they could spend time together talking violin and Russian. Heifetz, when making his famous recording of the Scottish Fantasy with Sargent, requested Sascha, who was attending the sessions, to sit a little further away, with the words, "It's not easy to conjure in front of a conjurer", and his affection for Lasserson is clear to see in a delightful photo of them together in which Heifetz is smiling broadly; a collector's piece.

Perhaps unusually for his age, Sascha was interested in modern music and kept abreast of the times; he thought there was a beauty in the [2nd] Bartok concerto, was moved by the Berg and, although he had not memorised them, knew both Prokofiev concerti backwards. He was always willing to listen to contemporary pieces and I can remember how pleased he was with himself when, during one of my lessons, he spotted a wrong note I was playing in an unaccompanied sonata by Martinon, which he had never before heard.

Of the old school, thank God, Sascha generally taught violin in hand and believed in playing for his pupils. He would demonstrate passages from a huge repertoire without so much as a glance at the score and it was only in the Paganini Caprices, for some reason, that his memory was beginning to fail. Not that he couldn't still rattle off all 24 of them by heart; he could; it's just that he occasionally had to be reminded as to which number went with which caprice! At the end of a lesson he would very often prop himself up against the mantelpiece – to alleviate the rheumatism – and sail through some of the most hair-raising virtuoso music ever written, with the Ernst *Erlkonig* and *Last Rose of Summer* being just two of them.

I enthused during a lesson one day about the winner of the Tchaikovsky Competition who had broadcast a performance of the Paganini concerto the night before. Sascha was less ecstatic: "When you've heard Heifetz at the age of 9 and Elman at the age of 10, it's hard to get excited." Besides, the soloist had committed the unforgivable sin of 'cutting' the most difficult section of the Sauret cadenza. I hadn't even known it was the Sauret cadenza. Sascha picked up his fiddle and began to play it; after a while he murmured, amidst dazzling fingerboard feats, "He cut from here" – another couple of minutes went by – "to here," and he gradually brought the cadenza to a close. An example of one-upmanship hard to beat!

There are many more anecdotes about Sascha Lasserson; all of them tell of an endearing human being and many of them point to the incredibly high position of respect in which he was held by the violin fraternity. There was hardly a fiddle player in London who hadn't been through Mr Lasserson's hands and once, while freelancing with the LPO, I discovered that every violinist on that gig had had lessons with him at some time or another!

My own debt to Sascha Lasserson is enormous. He gave me the tools with which I learned to play well and which have enabled me to go on improving. He gave me confidence in my own ability by nurturing my individuality, both musical and violinistic. I remember him every day. He is especially close to me now that teaching is a major part of my career, and I find it literally awe-inspiring to witness how successfully his principles and methods are benefiting my students. Since he kept his passion for the violin and enthusiasm for the teaching of it right to the end of his long life, I am sure Sascha would be thrilled to bits to know that his influence is now having such a positive effect on young violinists in north-west America.

Geoffrey Trabichoff began studying with Sascha Lasserson in 1968, when Sascha was 78. Leader of the BBC Scottish Symphony Orchestra from 1982-1997, he also led the Hanover State, Mannheim Chamber, and Gulbenkian Orchestras. Now Professor of Violin at Albertson College, Idaho, and Concertmaster of Boise Philharmonic Orchestra, he has appeared as a soloist and recitalist throughout Europe and north-west America.

Brian Underwood

As this is a collection of personal reminiscences of one of the most important and influential violinists to have graced the musical world of twentieth-century England, I hope I may be forgiven if occasionally, in the course of recall, I meander from the central figure of Sascha Lasserson in order to make an effort at placing him in perspective both historically as well as personally.

From a relatively early age I had heard the name of Lasserson – uttered in somewhat revered, often hushed tones, synonymous with all that was fine and pure in violin playing. One heard that Lasserson was a pupil of the great Leopold Auer; that Lasserson was a friend and fellow student of Heifetz and Elman, two of the most illustrious names on the concert platform, who were known to have such respect for Lasserson that they both made a point of meeting and playing to him when they were in London. It was also said that many of England's best known violinists had studied or were studying with Lasserson and that secretly some students from the London colleges were going to him for 'tips'. There was no doubt that Lasserson was someone special.

After a shaky start at six years old on a full sized violin (which was to cause me considerable and painful problems later) I was fortunate in becoming a pupil of a fine local Romford teacher, Alfred Jones. He was born in St Petersburg (where his father owned lemonade and ice-cream factories) and had studied the violin with Michael Serbulov, a pupil of Sevcik, Vieuxtemps and Wieniawski.

It was Alfred Jones who first fired my imagination with stories of Imperial Russia and of the events leading up to the October Revolution. He related an incident during the early days of the rebellion when, whilst queuing for bread, a group of over-excited Cossacks galloped through the streets firing at random, shooting dead a young woman queuing just in front of him. Soon after, he left with his family for Yokahama via Vladivostok, as the war in Europe made it impossible to return to England. He lived and played in Japan for two years before returning to London with the intention of studying with Ysaye. However, that great artist had returned to Belgium and Alfred Jones was advised by Hill's of Bond Street to study at the Royal College of Music with Maurice Sons. Although Sascha Lasserson had been in England for about six years, at that time he was still performing a great deal and was not yet established as the teacher with the renowned reputation which was to come later.

Alfred Jones had known Jascha Heifetz in St Petersburg and had translated letters in English received by the young virtuoso, mostly from America. I recall him telling me how comparatively impoverished the Heifetz family were; of his visiting Jascha at home where the living room contained little more than a grand piano which the young violinist had won in a competition, and of his friend playing to him informally with a technical perfection and beauty of tone he found spellbinding.

Alfred Jones loved the violin playing of St Petersburg. He loved the city and the country and held my awe-struck attention as he described the long, hard, snow-laden winters when horse-drawn, bell-jingling troikas sped along Nevsky Prospect, clouds of steam rising from the heads of the magnificent animals as their breath met the bitter cold air; being chased by wolves across the snowy plains; trying to perform the E minor Mozart sonata with frozen fingers, having left it too late for warming up after an ice-skating session, and of being reprimanded by his teacher Serbulov with a silence which he said was rather more effective than a verbal lashing.

But much of his discourse on life in St Petersburg was centred on the violin playing of the Auer pupils. It was from him I first heard the names of Heifetz, Elman, Lasserson, Poliakin, Toscha Seidel, Zimbalist, and Cecilia Hansen; and he described how, because Auer's room would not hold all who wanted to attend his class, many were forced to listen behind closed doors where they could still enjoy the beautiful sounds emanating from within. Beauty of tone coupled with tasteful and artistic use of vibrato.

When Alfred Jones died, his son very kindly presented me with his vast collection of music accumulated from his early studies in St Petersburg and beyond. Amongst this collection was a Russian dictionary of musical terms. In spite of my limited knowledge of Cyrillic the first word I deciphered as I opened the little book was 'vibrato'. My wife, Alla Sharova, translated the explanation, "an oscillation of the hand which must be used with great discretion." By this time I had spent four years at the Royal Academy of Music with Frederick Grinke and a period in Amsterdam as a member of that city's Philharmonic Orchestra. Whilst there I had studied with Oskar Back (an Ysaye pupil who, before becoming one of the youngest professors at the Vienna Conservatoire, had studied the violin repertoire of Brahms with the composer), and when Back died at the age of 84, with Steven Staryk who was then leader of the Concertgebouw.

All my teachers I admired and respected and I am grateful for their care, encouragement and inspiration. Back, Grinke and Steven Staryk all expressed a liking for my vibrato. I was never really convinced. I felt that the vibrato I had been encouraged to use at the Academy was developing into a poor imitation of Frederick Grinke's, which sounded excellent when he played, but was not right for me. Alfred Jones wouldn't have liked it either.

By the time I returned to England and began playing in the profession here, I was experiencing the need for independence – a desire to find greater freedom in my playing, freedom with discipline. I was working a great deal with Harry Blech's London Mozart Players, playing some of the music I enjoy most with excellent and delightful musicians. Several of these were for me household names, as I had been an avid listener to their frequent radio broadcasts from my early childhood. Playing in this, the Geraint Jones Orchestra and other leading chamber orchestras as well as the Philharmonia and BBC Symphony, I became aware of sharing desks with violinists who were able to play with considerable freedom within a disciplined ensemble sense and yet had a distinctive quality of style which identified a 'Lasserson' pupil. I liked their use of vibrato, too.

One of these fine players was the Australian-born Margot Macgibbon (founder and leader of the Macgibbon Quartet) with whom I travelled by car across the length and breadth of England for concerts when on tour with the Mozart Players. Margot enjoyed talking music and violin playing. So did I. She loaned me Auer's book, *My Long Life in Music*, and she spoke warmly of Sascha Lasserson, as did my friend and pianist, Valerie Pardon, who was also at that time playing with Geoffrey Trabichoff. Valerie had met and worked with Mr Lasserson at Geoffrey's lessons.

The names of Editha Knocker (the Auer pupil who translated Leopold Mozart's book into English), Auer and of course Sascha all seemed to pop like firecrackers from Margot's conversation, and it was not long before she was giving me Lasserson's telephone number, with the words, "Sascha is very good if you know what you want." I dialled, hardly able to comprehend the fact that the line was ringing and that I might actually be speaking within a few seconds to someone who was already to me a legend. Eventually the great man answered. I mentioned Margot. He suggested a date and a time. "I am at 53 Stern Street," he said. "You know the violinist Isaac Stern? – Stern Street."

One gloriously sunny summer afternoon I arrived at the front door of Bunty Lempfert's corner house in Shepherds Bush. A few moments after the appointed time Mr Lasserson appeared from a side door, inviting me to follow him into the artists' studio which stood in the rear garden of the house. Little did I know that this was to be the beginning of a wonderfully happy period of my life, which was to include a teacher/pupil relationship with Sascha Lasserson, which became a friendship of trust and which produced, over a period of nine years, a catalogue of delightful memories.

At this first encounter he seemed very reserved and rather serious. I could sense him assessing me even before I played as he peered at me over the top of his very small, circular, almost Pickwickian spectacles. His jacket hung over the back of a chair, but he still wore his suit waistcoat and tie in spite of the heat of the day. Even then he made me feel I wanted to play to him – odd, for someone who was always very nervous. He looked at my hands; I looked at his, so incredibly large and strong for a person of such small physique – by comparison mine looked like uncooked spaghetti. I played the Bach E major Prelude and the slow movement of the Beethoven concerto. I don't remember if he stopped me or if he allowed me to finish, but when he spoke I became immediately aware of the twinkle in his eye and the directness when he said, "You are a good musician – any particular problems?" And before I could answer he said, "You are a bit stiff, yes?" I agreed. I did not mention vibrato. He did. "You have good vibrato but you use too much all the time. You remind me of ..." And he mentioned the name of a well-known quartet. "I cannot listen to them; I have to switch off the radio when I try to listen to their broadcasts. Too much vibrato." Auer would say, "Café restaurant players." I remembered reading of Auer's own experience when, as a teenager, he played to Vieuxtemps, who was on tour in Hungary. Believing himself to be playing with great expression, he was so devastated at Madam Vieuxtemps' search for the cat she was sure was locked in somewhere and of the master's comment, "Never mind, my boy, you might improve," that he fainted. Auer disliked excessive vibrato ever after. I did not faint. I remembered Alfred Jones' words, "We must not sound like Lyons Corner House players." I understood what Mr Lasserson meant, for I had come full circle. I was again to hear first-hand accounts of St Petersburg before the Revolution, its culture, and its art of violin playing.

There are of course many excellent café restaurant players who are fine musicians in their own right and have decided or have been forced by circumstances to specialise in salon or light music. It was, perhaps sadly, the fashion at the turn of the century and even until fairly recently to classify anyone who played this music as being inferior to the broadly classical player. However, what violinist could fail to be impressed by the sheer brilliance and talent of the Budapest 'gypsies' and many other European and our own light music players, who often play with such a fine sense of style and line? Or not warm to the wonderfully talented and refined communicator Max Jaffa, a devoted Lasserson pupil who has written so appreciatively of his debt to Sascha in his autobiography *A Life on the Fiddle*.

What Messrs Jones and Lasserson meant, of course, was that one should avoid excess – going over the top. Yet, whilst it may have been a hundred years ago, it was principally the salon musicians who were accused of this trend (possibly just because the audiences they played for demanded it). They would hardly be isolated now, judging by the presentation of some of today's new names in the classical world.

Lasserson liked elegance, good taste, purity of line and musical style and he tried to instil these qualities into his pupils whilst encouraging them to be themselves, to be expansive and to play with freedom. Lasserson and Alfred Jones were born into an era when the aristocracy – the nobility – ruled in Russia. Peter the Great founded his gateway to the West, bringing from there the best architects, draftsmen and craftsmen of all kinds to help build St Petersburg, generally famed for its aesthetic beauty; and then later, with the furnishing by the nobility of many of the most magnificent buildings with some of the finest works of art from Europe and around the world, an environment was created which must surely have influenced the tastes of those fortunate to live there. This environment was, musically speaking, further enriched when the Empress Anna in 1731 invited singers and musicians from Italy to provide music for her court functions. Until the end of the eighteenth century a series of Italian violinists – several distinguished pupils of the great masters including Vivaldi, Tartini and Nardini – were to exert the first foreign influence on violin playing in Russia, followed from the time of the French Revolution by a series of French violinists active at the St Petersburg court, usually holding the title of 'soloist to the Tsar'. Two of these musicians, Rode and his pupil Lafont, displayed qualities of elegance much admired by their patrons.

Since French was the language of the court, it is not surprising that, even around the time of Napoleon's abortive invasion, the style and technique of the French School of violin playing was encouraged by the nobility; and that this, together with many other foreign influences too, evolved into what became known by the end of the nineteenth century as 'The Russian School'. Hence Lasserson's assertion that there is no such thing as "The Russian School"! Even the highly esteemed Polish violinist, Wieniawski, soloist to the Tsar and first professor of violin at the St Petersburg Conservatoire who preceded Leopold Auer in both posts, had studied in Paris for fourteen years from the age of eight, with the aid of a Russian scholarship.

Upon succeeding Wieniawski, Auer taught diligently for thirty years before the culmination of his long experience found his class imbued with the array of outstanding talent we remember today.

Many of these were of Jewish origin, who came to St Petersburg from the areas of the pogroms. They were fortunate in coming to the attention of Auer, for he was in a position to secure permission for them to reside, usually with at least one close member of their families, in a city which was, at that time, closed to all but the most talented Jews. Lasserson's first Conservatoire professor, Nikolai Galkin, was also able to obtain support for his seven-year-old protégé from Vitebsk. By the time Lasserson entered Auer's class at the age of ten, many of those destined for fame were already there. Heifetz came a little later, Milstein when Lasserson was already in England.

Although the great Auer pupils were and are recognisable by their qualities in terms of style, intonation and tone shading, each played with a unique character and often with a charm which was decidedly their own. Lasserson's extraordinary sensitivity as well as his almost magical control of the bow are clearly demonstrated in his only known recording of a snippet of the Dvorak/Kreisler E minor *Slavonic Dance*. But we all remember his playing to us at lessons. He made everything look and sound so easy, so simple, so uncomplicated. Just as Milstein's unassuming reply to Pinchas

Zuckerman, who asked him, "How do you make the G minor *Sicilienne* of Bach sound so beautiful?" was, "I try not to spoil it". So was Lasserson's approach to his art – unassuming and logical. Perhaps this was the key to his greatness for, as Mozart was able to present us with a phrase which can be so easily understood and yet is so dumbfoundedly hallmarked with genius, Lasserson was able to make a point in violin playing. Many excellent examples have already been given in this collection. He was never pedantic, avoided repetition, and did not try to be clever; he had no need to try, he was. As with all truly great teachers, it was not just his talent and considerable knowledge, gained from his own education and later experience, that gave us so much in the way of improving our violin playing. It was the man himself, his original personality, his spirit and his soul which will live on in the hearts and minds of all who knew him. He was influenced to an extent by his colleagues and by his own fine teachers, but these influences did not make Lasserson; for he was always his own man, able to assess objectively players of the past, the present and, frequently, the future.

I have often wondered if he would have survived so long if he had been obliged only to perform. There is no doubt that teaching was for him a vocation. He once told me his father had been a Rabbi and that it was from him he had inherited his love of teaching. Lasserson's passion was not just to impart knowledge but also to inspire his pupils to seek answers for themselves. Like his brother Simeon, of whom he spoke often, and two of his sisters, Sascha Lasserson was dedicated to the care and education of the young and all who needed help.

"You cannot learn how to play the violin from books," he once said to me as we walked together from the studio to his bus stop at Shepherds Bush Green. I had been relaying to him my pleasure at reading the uncomplicated writing of Auer in his book *The Violin As I Teach It*. "Auer says in that book that the left thumb is not important, but the thumb is very important." He was referring to Auer's reference to foreign students seeking his advice about the left thumb. Auer writes that he told them to forget the thumb, presumably to prevent them becoming too self-conscious about it, a technique often also used by Lasserson and with great effect.

He felt my own interest in analysing violinistic problems was inhibiting my playing, and so he said, "When you know too much, it becomes difficult to play." Then he quoted Carl Flesch who, in his thesis on technique, had written that the best bow hold was that of the Russian School. Soon after its publication, Lasserson was inundated with requests for instruction on how Auer taught the bow hold. "I had to bluff," he told me. "I couldn't remember." When Cecilia Hansen next visited London from her home in Germany the two friends and colleagues met for lunch. Lasserson told Hansen of his dilemma – so many violinists were asking him how Auer taught the bow hold. Could she remember? But Cecilia Hansen had found herself in a similar predicament in her adopted homeland. She had also been unable to remember and, having consulted with other Auer pupils, it was collectively agreed that Auer had said nothing on this particular point. Not even the position of the index finger? I suggested to Mr Lasserson that perhaps the distinctive bow hold may have possibly evolved from a combination of the successful 'chemistry' which existed between teacher and pupil; their mutual talent, and sensitivity to style and tone production. After a few moments' thought he said, "That is probably right."

I found his psychology in teaching of the highest calibre. He was able to respond quickly with just the right phrase to make you pull yourself together or to encourage you. Working over a period of some time through Ernst's *Otello* and *Hungarian Fantasies*, the F# minor concerto and *Die Letzte Rose*, I dared to suggest that a particular passage was tricky. "Tricky?" he retorted. "Nonsense. Heifetz played this when he was ten." I did not complain again and much later made a point of including some of these pieces in recitals. I am greatly indebted to Mr Lasserson for introducing me to Ernst as I find his material extremely valuable for attaining better control in the music of the standard composers.

He was aware of my need to play with ever greater freedom and would say, "My favourite violinist was Ysaye; such a big player –

huge man about six feet tall – played E major prelude with almost the whole bow on every note. Even Jascha was by comparison small." Lasserson loved and admired the genius of Heifetz but was quick to prevent any slavish imitation of even that paragon. He did not encourage me to listen to any violinists but he did advise me to listen to a singer – one singer – Dietrich Fischer-Dieskau. Lasserson held Albert Sammons in high esteem not least because he believed him to be largely self taught and was very proud of a letter he had received from the eminent English violinist in the 20s expressing his admiration for Lasserson's broadcast performances of the Beethoven Sonatas.

He admired Milstein's purity of tone and, when that virtuoso was playing at the Festival Hall, he was very keen that I should meet him. Lasserson was unable to attend on that occasion as his wife was unwell but he insisted that I "go round afterwards" and introduce myself. Alla too was unable to attend, and so it was with even more trepidation than that experienced before my first meeting with Lasserson that I made my way to the Green Room. After a magnificent and inspired performance of the Beethoven concerto, I was greeted by a gentleman of great charm and humour. He was delighted to receive the message I brought from his old friend and asked immediately after Mrs Lasserson, whom Milstein knew to be in poor health.

The last time Lasserson was to hear Milstein in public was at the Festival Hall where he again played the Beethoven; Lasserson was adamant that Alla and I should accompany him backstage after the performance. The two Auer pupils spoke in English. Alla asserts that both were still masters of their mother tongue, but their touchingly good manners from a sadly bygone age would never allow them to breach their sense of etiquette by launching into Russian, of which my knowledge was and sadly still is limited. Milstein told us about a back problem from which he had been suffering for some time. "My doctor said it will help if I go down on one knee – but how can I do that on the concert platform?" "You know," replied Lasserson, who was then suffering from severe rheumatism, "when I have a pain in my shoulder, I play the Chaconne of Bach and the pain goes." Milstein, clearly moved, allowed his friend Lasserson the last word.

When, after Lasserson's death, Alla and I were guests of Nathan Milstein and his beautiful wife Thérèse, at their house in Chester Square, the veteran violinist spoke to me of his great admiration for both Oskar Back and Sascha Lasserson. He regarded them as two of the finest and most important pedagogues in Europe. Milstein said, "With Back I talked music, with Lasserson I talked violin. Lasserson was not only a wonderful violinist and teacher, but also a wonderful person."

On the occasion of Sascha Lasserson's 85th birthday, Alla and I were invited to tea with the Lassersons at their flat in St Quintin Avenue. Lionel Bentley was there, too. He had just been appointed a professor at the Royal Academy of Music. Lasserson told him, "The trouble with the Academy – they don't teach enough Spohr concertos" – a sentiment voiced by other international pedagogues and one which hopefully may one day be properly addressed. Lasserson and his colleagues believed that a violinist's true foundation lay for a large part in the preparation of the 'study' concertos by the violinist composers such as Spohr, Kreutzer, Rode and Viotti.

Contemplating the thorough grounding Lasserson and his colleagues had in these works even before entering Auer's class, I am reminded of Lasserson recalling and relating an incident which occurred at the age of seven when he was studying with Galkin. Galkin had asked his young pupil to prepare the Kreutzer D major concerto. Lasserson's father, on noting the piece to be practised, gave his son the Rode number seven, saying, "Take this – much better." Sascha, responding to his father's bidding, prepared the Rode, duly arrived for his next lesson and placed the music on the stand. Galkin, a very large being, stood on the far side of the room. Sascha was making ready to play close to the third-floor window. It was mid-winter and very cold. Galkin, on observing the 'wrong' piece, leapt across the room, took the small, terrified boy by the scruff of the neck, carried him swiftly to the window which he opened and then proceeded to hold him dangling outside three floors up, for some seconds. Upon bringing Sascha back inside he said, "The next time you bring me the wrong piece I will do the same but I will let you go." With that the boy was sent packing from the room together with music and stand. Galkin forgave him and some days later, on meeting Sascha in the corridor, asked him if he would like a lesson. On a subsequent occasion Lasserson remembered Galkin stopping his carriage when he noticed Sascha walking along the street with a fellow Galkin pupil. Calling Sascha over he gave him sweets, saying, "Don't give any to him," gesturing towards the other boy, "he is a very rude young man."

Perhaps the sequel to the former Galkin story was related to me by a colleague who, whilst on tour with the London Philharmonic Orchestra in the States, met an American concertmaster, a former Auer pupil. He had studied in St Petersburg at the same time as Sascha Lasserson who, he recalled, was the only pupil in the class always ready with at least three major works when everyone else was lucky to have prepared one. When Auer asked him what he was going to play, the choice of three would be given but with the question, "Which one would you like, Professor?" Lasserson himself enjoyed telling anecdotes from his St Petersburg days which, he once told me, were for him the happiest of times. There was never any hint of malice in any of the stories he intentionally told to display the human frailties of even the greatest. One of these described his arrival at the Conservatoire on the morning following an evening concert at which Leopold Auer had played the Mendelssohn concerto, but which Lasserson was unable to attend. A formidable gathering of violinists, many of them Auer pupils, were huddled together in the entrance hall whispering excitedly. One of them came over to Lasserson asking, "Have you heard the news?" "News?" he enquired, expecting to hear something of the gravest nature, "What news?" He was told, "Last night Auer played the octaves out of tune."

Lasserson helped co-ordinate all I had learned from my previous teachers and encouraged me to do what I felt was 'right' both in playing and teaching. He convinced me of the importance of trying to listen and to assess with the utmost objectivity. He believed you should hear a player many times before forming a definite opinion. "Sometimes," he said, "a good player sounds bad and a bad player sounds good." His ability to make a molehill out of a mountain was often astonishing in its simplicity. I arrived for my lesson one day presumably looking shattered for he asked, "What's the matter? What have you been doing?" I told him I had come from a chamber music rehearsal and that we had been working so hard at intonation, I no longer knew what I was doing. I had been taught, from an early age, that violin intonation was relative unless you are playing with the piano when it must often be tempered. I had also been encouraged – in fact I enjoyed – finding the Tartini Tones in double stops. "What should we be aiming for in the quartet?" I asked him. "Tempered, relative, what?" He replied simply and very quietly, "Intonation is a sixth sense." At once all was clear. It had nothing to do with intellect but instinct, and of course training your fingers to respond to that sixth sense and sometimes just trying to fit in with what is going on around you when playing with others. Trying to make it sound 'right'.

Much later when we played through the Bach double together, he said when we had finished, "Well, at least we played in tune." I still don't know if he was matching me or I was matching him, any more than I know whether, when he said I played the Tchaikovsky like an Auer pupil, he meant one of those at Auer's class who was told to sit down and never allowed to play!

Although it was a great privilege to study the Glazunov with one of the few who had played it with the composer conducting, it is the Tchaikovsky concerto which will always bring back the most stimulating memories of a superb artist. For I have heard no one play this work more beautifully or with more conviction. I was present, too, when he worked through this concerto with Alla and was fascinated by the fine graceful bowing of the two St Petersburg players and the 'rightness' of their interpretations.

He rarely paid compliments unless it was to emphasise an aspect of one's playing that was 'special'. In my case, it was staccato. "Any kind of staccato," he said, "you can do firm up bow, down bow, flying, stationary, arpeggiando, the lot." The responsibility of trying to be in form with these strokes just in case Mr Lasserson asked for a demonstration was enormous, and it certainly kept the adrenaline flowing as I was always afraid of disappointing him. This is a light-hearted matter but important because this personal technique of his helped to fuse a happy and relaxed relationship with his pupils, and encouraged a joyful feeling for the magic and the romance of the violin. This balanced well with his more profound ideas, awareness, and insight into the music.

Mindful of these qualities, it was with the warmest of feelings that one left after a lesson at which Mr Lasserson had intimated satisfaction with an interpretation. On one such occasion I played him the slow movement of the Brahms concerto. It was, for me, a 'good day', and when the final note had faded, he came over to me, smiled, and without saying a word, applauded. He had the gift of making us all feel that we were important to him. One Sunday morning the telephone rang. I answered. A familiar voice said, "Lasserson here. Are you all right? I haven't seen you for some time." I explained that I had been very busy with rehearsals and concerts for some weeks but was looking forward to my next lesson. "What are you going to bring?" he enquired. I told him that, when I could, I was practising Bach, Ernst, scales and the Tchaikovsky concerto. "Is that all?" he said with just a hint of an amused chuckle. I could almost hear him thinking what he had said on occasions when showing me letters with requests for lessons with complete CVs containing vast lists of works studied: "Well, if one can play all those, one doesn't need lessons."

I tried only once to seek his help with one of my own pupils. A small and very talented girl was finding extensions in first position especially awkward even though the instrument was not too large for her. "Tell her to play in 2nd position," was his very logical suggestion. The only further advice he gave me when I asked if he would check some of my pupils was, "You know how to teach, you don't need my help. Just remember, not all problems are violinistic. Sometimes they are medical and need the attention of a medical specialist." Also, "Don't waste time with pupils who have interfering parents. However talented, they will come to nothing. It isn't worth it."

I have long believed that his philosophy of teaching was revealed when he said to Averil Carmalt, "I try to stand in the shoes of the pupil and assess the problems from the pupil's point of view." And when he said to me, "You know, it is very satisfying when you can help someone to play something who couldn't play anything." This was said after the lesson, which preceded mine, of a gentleman in his sixties who had just given a creditable account of Tartini's *Didona Abandonata*. He had been a beginner only twelve months earlier, and Lasserson had agreed to take such a late starter on condition he practised one hour every day. The result was astonishing.

I found his imagination for Bach fascinating and convincing. It seems inconceivable that the composer, who was so alert to all styles of musical self-expression of his time, did not explore the music of the synagogue too. Is it not possible that the composing of the unaccompanied Sonatas and Partitas was influenced by the glorious timbres and augmented intervals sung by the Cantor?

Lasserson loved his pupils as he loved his family and spoke of both with pride and affection. When I asked him if nothing could be done for his beloved wife Zelda, who was suffering from a serious heart condition, he spoke of the five doctors in his family – one a distinguished heart specialist – who had all offered a poor prognosis. He was distraught when she died, but after many months during which he told me he practised mostly Bach, he said, "I think I am getting better. You know, most of my colleagues are already playing the harp but I still play the violin."

The heart specialist was his nephew, Cecil Symons, a fine person of enormous intelligence and sensitivity who, together with Margot Macgibbon and W. E. Hill & Sons, became an official founder of the Sascha Lasserson Memorial Trust (currently donating annually to the Junior Departments of the four main London music colleges).

I read with considerable pleasure accounts from other Lasserson pupils of the episodes with the gas fire at the Bayswater Studio. This was long before my studies with him. However, the fact of his being clearly an excellent shot was confirmed by Cecil Symons' sister, Pat Sussman. She recalled their being taken as children by Uncle Sascha to the local fair, every bank holiday at Wormwood Scrubs, where he was invariably asked to leave the rifle range, having shot all the ducks the first time round. But his favourite game apparently was darts which he would play standing poised on his toes, taking aim "just like Eros", the children would say, and then inevitably scoring a bullseye. They never arrived home without several goldfish.

The Lassersons lived in the top floor flat of a house in which there was no lift and Sascha had to descend several flights each time the doorbell rang. On the occasion of his seventy-fifth birthday, Pat was bewailing the lack of official recognition at the end of a day which had brought an inordinate number of rings from below. "Never mind, Sascha, there's no doubt you will go to Paradise," she told him. "I hope not," he retorted, "they might give me another top floor flat!" Pat Sussman also related an incident that Sascha had told her of a particular visit to his local off-licence where he went regularly to buy his cigarettes. The previous evening the BBC had broadcast the British premiere of a Shostakovich symphony. The shop owner was a keen music lover and, on seeing Lasserson enter, called welcomingly across the shop, "Good evening, Mr Lasserson. What did you think of the Shostakovich? Wasn't it terrific?" "It was," replied Mr Lasserson, upon which a customer at the counter said, "If it's that good, I'll try a bottle!"

I have always enjoyed recalling his account of an incident, when he waited at a bus stop, violin case in hand and a rather small elderly lady, also carrying a violin, arrived and stood next to him. "You play the violin, too?" she asked. "Yes, I do," came the polite but reserved reply. "I was a pupil of Sauret," she informed him with obvious pride. At that moment Lasserson's bus arrived and he had to leave her. He told me with more than just a twinge of impish humour, "I wanted to ask her if she could play the Sauret cadenza of the Paganini" (which Lasserson himself played so brilliantly).

During the final years, when he began to find the journey to Bunty's studio too tiring, he taught at home. My lesson was usually the last of the afternoon and when it was over he would often invite me to stay for tea. This would be brought in by his son, Michael, who had given up his job to care for his father after the death of Mrs Lasserson. Michael would eventually leave us and, with Leopold Auer and his illustrious disciples looking down from the photograph which stood on the piano, Alexander Lvovich, as I by then called him (in the polite form I had become used to when addressing my wife's parents and older Russian friends) would talk at great length about violin playing, music and St Petersburg. He remembered Elman's arrival in St Petersburg at about the same time as the outstanding Hungarian child prodigy, Ferenc Vecsey, was scheduled to play the Mendelssohn concerto. Elman was taken to the rehearsal and during the interval, after the Mendelssohn, strolled among the orchestral players on the platform. On being asked his impressions of such a wonderful player, he replied rather cheekily, "I play it better than that." He was naturally chided by the adults and, metaphorically speaking, elbowed and kicked off the platform. On that same platform some months later Elman himself stood – playing the Mendelssohn. All had to admit – it was better.

Lasserson would speak, too, of the comparatively limited training in England offered to violinists, and declared that although there was no shortage of talent in this country, as soon as anyone stands up to say what needs to be done, they are pushed down by the majority. His opinion of Associated Board exams was not high. If he was asked to prepare a pupil for their examinations, he would say, "I don't teach Associated Board – I teach the violin."

He would try to persuade me to 'do a Wigmore' and I told him circumstances made it impossible. Then he would say, "You must do the pools." When I said, "But nobody would come," he assured me, "I'll come and I will tell all my pupils to come, too." Such was the kindness and encouragement he bestowed on countless pupils who were fortunate enough to understand his message. There were exceptions and of those he would say, "You don't have to tell anyone they will never be any good. Just teach them properly, and they will leave".

He would take me over to the piano and direct my attention to that famous photograph, pointing out Elman, Burgin, Piastro, the very pretty Cecilia Hansen and himself sitting elegantly in the front row, second from left. The face strong, the eyes gentle – is there just the hint of a suppressed smile (they all had to keep very still) hardly masking that puck-like humour I experienced at many heart-warming moments? Once, during a discourse on presentation, he proceeded to demonstrate how the great violinists of his day walked on to the platform. I wish my memory was as good as his and that I could recall in detail the various characteristics and mannerisms of each individual he portrayed on that delightful occasion. But I do remember that his impression of Kubelik was a hoot and I was almost reduced to tears from laughter. Again, he intimated not the slightest degree of malice. Nor was there a hint of malice when he said, "Did you hear Elman play on television?" I hadn't. Lasserson went on to say, "He phoned me after his performance and asked my opinion. What could I say? On that occasion, he had played as if he had just come from the synagogue. I did not tell him." But he did tell us that as highly as he revered his friend, whose tone he said was larger even than their teacher's, Lasserson did not feel Elman had studied long enough with Auer.

Lasserson never made an issue of being Jewish in spite of the history of his own birthplace. "I've heard it said," he told me, "that you need the temperament of a Jew to play the violin well. But I have Jewish pupils with no temperament and non-Jewish pupils with too much."

Lasserson was a truly good man. Nona Liddell once referred to him as a saint. Saintly he most certainly was, and the Jewish faith would have no hesitation in allowing this Zaddik into Paradise. However, as the Jewish faith has no harp-playing angels, it is unlikely Lasserson will be playing that instrument. But is there any doubt that he is still playing the violin and charming all around him with the music we loved to hear him play?

My very last instruction from Alexander Lvovich was in fact when he corrected my Russian. As I was leaving him after a stimulating session on the Ysaye *Ballade*, we both said, "dosvidanya" (until we meet again) and he added, "bud'te zdorovi" (be healthy). I responded with the familiar term used at home, "bud zdorov." He called me back. "You say 'bud zdorov' to a little boy but to me it should be 'bud'te zdorovi'. You know," he continued, "a very young girl pupil of mine, about eighteen, wrote me a postcard from holiday which began 'Dear Sascha'. When she returned I told her I'm not Sascha, I am Mr Lasserson."

I left him standing on his top floor landing, having apologised for my error, and after a final shake of that strong warm hand we both said, "bud'te zdorovi, dosvidanya" and he gave me a final wave as I looked back from the bottom of the first flight of stairs. Whether we knew him as Sascha, Alexander Lvovich or Mr Lasserson, we all share wonderful memories of happy times spent with a great talent who was our link with our history and who was a trusted mentor and friend.

Brian Underwood studied with Frederick Grinke at the Academy, and then with Oskar Bach and Steven Staryk in Amsterdam, where he was a member of the Amsterdam Philharmonic. He was a member of the London Mozart Players and Geraint Jones Orchestra and the European Masterplayers, as well as a freelance with most of the London orchestras. He now teaches violin and ensemble playing at the Junior Academy and North-West London Collegiate School.

He studied with Sascha Lasserson for many years, and has been very actively involved in the running of the Lasserson Memorial Trust ever since its inception, as well as the Lasserson Competitions. He has performed as recitalist and ensemble player both in England and abroad, and his teaching experience has included involvement with master-classes at both the Delhi and Calcutta Schools of Music. Many of his pupils are currently enjoying active and successful careers in the music profession.

Anne Warden

I still remain honoured, after so many years, by my time spent studying with Sascha. He, as artist and teacher, added so much insight and inspiration to my lengthy career in solo playing.

His wonderful playing of the Bach solo sonatas was indeed a revelation, as was also his playing of the Paganini caprices.

I remain ever grateful to him, and now, at a time when I am no longer able to play the violin because of arthritis, I am greatly consoled by memories of Sascha's kindness and humanity.

Tessa Wilkinson

It was an old friend, John Ludlow (whom I had known many years earlier at the RCM), who advised me to go to Sascha Lasserson at a time when I had finally decided that I must seek help with my playing. I had been teaching the violin to children and, while I was well aware of my problems, I felt far too nervous to play to anybody. John reassured me, saying "Nobody is frightened of Sascha," at the same time explaining that Sascha had done a lot of what he – John – called 'repair work'!

Eventually, in April 1976, I turned up at the Studio in Shepherd's Bush where Sascha did much of his teaching, and met him for the first time. He agreed to teach me, saying, "Everybody calls me Sascha." I had only a few lessons at Shepherd's Bush, going after that to his flat in North Kensington.

I explained that, above all things, I wanted to learn how to play unaccompanied Bach – and was at once privileged to hear an amazing performance of the *Chaconne*. Sascha's interpretative powers were as amazing as his memory, and his playing had an ease and elegance which I could only admire but never hope to achieve. I felt I was entering into the great traditions of the Russian Violin School.

I discovered that Sascha particularly enjoyed his birthday celebrations, when pupils would bring gifts of flowers and chocolates; in return he would make tea – refusing all offers of help, and of course he smoked continually with a little trail of ash falling down his suit. He told me how, when he was studying with Auer, the very young Heifetz came to play – giving an astonishing performance of the Mendelssohn concerto that forced Auer to break his own rule never to take pupils of such an age, and so Heifetz was accepted into the class. Sascha also told of an occasion when he had been the supporting artist at a recital given by

Clara Butt. She was extremely put out when his performance of the Kreisler-Corelli variations on *La Folia* brought him a standing ovation which eclipsed her own efforts! Again, he told me how much he admired Albert Sammons and how much he owed to him for, when the war started, Sammons passed several of his pupils to Sascha.

Any achievement by one of his pupils was something of which Sascha was very proud, and he made great efforts to attend his pupils' recitals. He used to say that they always played better if they knew he was there, and I am sure that they gained great reassurance from his affection for them and his confidence in their abilities.

My last lesson with him was on Saturday 1st July 1978, and this must have been one of the very last lessons he ever gave. I looked upon Sascha as a precious jewel hidden from most of the world but whose value – to those lucky enough to find him – was immeasurable.

Tessa Wilkinson studied at the RCM, first with Henry Holst and then with Marie Wilson, but illness prevented her graduating and taking up a career in music. Some twenty years later she resumed playing and was advised by friends to approach Sascha Lasserson for lessons. She studied with him until his death.

Trevor Williams

I had studied with several excellent teachers at the Royal Academy of Music; Sydney Robjohns, Harold Fairhurst and, particularly, David Martin, who gave me needed discipline after the faults I had acquired during two years without lessons (at the beginning of the Second World War) were at their worst.

I had begun to make my way in the profession and enjoyed eight years in the Aeolian Quartet, where I learned a great deal. When, in 1961, Heifetz recorded the Bruch *Scottish Fantasy*, Vieuxtemps 5th Concerto and the Bach Double with Erick Friedman at Walthamstow, I was fortunate to be playing in the orchestra and, although I had been to his concerts a few times before, it was thrilling to see him in action and at short range. I realised that I didn't know enough. Heifetz was one of the greatest violinists because of his extraordinary combination of genius and the knowledge and mastery brought about by organised and dedicated work.

Sascha Lasserson had known him since he was ten and said that the only person he heard play better than him now was Heifetz when he was younger. Sascha had studied with Auer in St Petersburg from 1900 to 1914 and had been present in the classes for all the best students of that time – Elman, Parlow, Achron, Borisov, Piastro, Poliakin, Hansen, Zimbalist (though he did not see Milstein, who came later, and who became a great friend when he visited England in the thirties).

Sascha himself won the Gold Medal – rarely awarded, and against the highest competition – at the St Petersburg Conservatoire. The award was for the performance from memory, and chosen by lottery of one of the six Bach Solo Sonatas. All had to be prepared, and Sascha said modestly, "I was lucky and drew the D minor." As a sign of the respect in which he was held, Heifetz said jokingly to him when he came to hear a concert of his, "What are you doing here? You've heard me play before. Does one conjuror play to another?"

I had decided to enter for the Thibaud Competition and asked Mr Lasserson to help me prepare for it. This he did, but it was too soon, and I did not go further than the first round. However, much more importantly, he showed me ways to improve, and in a kindly and often humorous and patient way he gave confidence, because, instead of playing being akin to Russian roulette, one learned to be able to rely on oneself – with exercises, scales, particularly in broken thirds and in four octaves, thirds, sixths and octaves, and the Dont *Caprices*, Paganini and Ernst. Sascha retained the ability to play all his old war horses until the end. I heard him when I went to see him a month before his death, at the age of eighty-eight!

I was grateful for all my teachers' help in the past, but it was Sascha who gave me what I needed most of all. He had many stories about his lessons with Auer, of playing Glazunov's concerto with the composer and he knew all the works of the romantic era. He described an occasion when Heifetz and Elman were beginning their return journey on the same train after playing in London in the same week, probably in the twenties or thirties. Elman had many friends to see him off, and Heifetz was alone at the other end of the train. Sascha was talking to each in turn, and said, "Why don't you travel together, you have the same background, the same teacher, why not go together ...?" "He goes his way, I go mine," said Heifetz.

Auer insisted that his students should be able to play anything they had done with him at any time. Kathleen Parlow, whom I met once, told me he said, "If I get you up in the morning at three you should be able to play!" Students were literally pushed or thrown out of the room if they were not prepared. Sascha himself would stop one playing by taking one arm or the other and, looking up under his brows (he was not a tall man), he would say, "You must have a repertoire!"

His remedies for problems were simple, like home hints, and if you 'set' yourself properly the difficulties were like fences in show-jumping and the results could be relied upon. However, his musical sense and knowledge of performance was also first class.

He was a great teacher, and had the humility of a great man. He was a source of encouragement to us all, and we loved him because he helped us find an instinctive way to express music, through the violin. Most of all, he was a wonderful man, and Max Jaffa told me that when he was despondent, at the end of the war, when Sascha saw him in absolute despair, he gave him lessons for a long period. Max felt he literally owed his life to Sascha's kindness and interest, while Sascha said Max was one of his most talented pupils.

We can all bear witness to his generosity of spirit, and will never forget him.

Trevor Williams studied at the RAM with David Martin, and subsequently with Sascha Lasserson for fourteen years. He was for eight years a member of the Aeolian Quartet and was appointed Concertmaster of the BBC Scottish and later the BBC Symphony Orchestra. He has been a Professor at the RAM since 1969, has coached the NYO, taught at Pro-Corda and conducted chamber orchestras. He now teaches privately, and conducts the Tudor Symphony Orchestra, an amateur group based in Finchley.

Sascha: a discussion

This is an edited transcript of a discussion among old pupils and relatives of Sascha recorded at the home of Kay and Emanuel Hurwitz (KH and EH). Those present were Lionel Bentley (LB), Tessa Robbins (TR), Nona Liddell (NL), Trevor Williams (TW), David Lasserson (DL) and Michael Lasserson (ML). The discussion was recorded by David van Dyl.

KH I remember Alan Bush, in whose orchestra Sascha used to play just after the war, describing Sascha's determination to get every note absolutely right – and his distress if he could not achieve that. He would hold up rehearsals in his endeavours, and really was quite unsuited to orchestral playing – where so often one just thribbles through. So he and Alan agreed that orchestral playing really was not his field – and they parted the very best of friends.

EH And yet he was forced, out of necessity, to do commercial work. I'm sure that during the war he led the orchestra in one of those corny musicals like Song of Norway – all about Grieg. I can remember playing with him in the on-stage band, in Don Giovanni at Covent Garden in 1938, with both of us dressed up in 18th century costume!

TW It was Max Jaffa who said he owed everything to Sascha because, after six years of war service in the Air Force, he could no longer play. He was almost suicidal with depression, until he met Sascha and persuaded him to give him lessons as one would a beginner. Sascha taught him for nothing, for about two years, and Max owed everything to him. Sascha was extraordinarily kind, with a generosity of spirit you don't always find – even among fine teachers.

NL He was never effusive with his praise but if you were unhappy and depressed he got so stressed himself because he couldn't bear to see people despondent. If he came to a concert, he would twinkle at you and say, "Very good! Could do better." But if you were miserable yourself, he would turn himself inside out to restore your confidence.

TR He never advertised. Really, he sat in his little bare room and people came by word of mouth. He really was not appreciated by the Establishment.

TW Which of us was the first to meet him?

LB Me! By a long way – very soon after he came to England. As a teenager, I was playing in one of the Lyons Corner House bands. I had no teacher, and the man who sold us strings advised me to go to Sascha – of whom I'd never heard. I went to play to him, and felt a nervous wreck because I could hear such fine playing from another pupil at his lesson. Anyway, Sascha heard me and took me on. I was with him for five years.

TW He was very proud of the Gold Medal he won at the St Petersburg Conservatory. This wasn't a yearly competition, because there were only about two or three ever awarded. The candidates had to prepare all the Bach sonatas and be ready to play whichever was selected for them. Sascha used to say, "I was lucky. I got the D Minor." And he won it. Milstein studied with Auer, after Sascha had left the Conservatoire, and when he came to England he met Sascha and said, "I've heard of you!" They were friends from then on.

It seems inconceivable that somebody could already have the beginnings of such a career back in Russia, then arrive here and somehow just melt into the landscape. But he did such wonderful work – behind the scenes. Everybody went to him.

KH He really wasn't the sort of person to push himself or try to sell himself.

LB I remember that big studio he rented in Finchley Road – he used to have students' concerts, with David Bor as the accompanist. I used to be terrified, but it was marvellous to hear all the other students play what they'd been studying with him. I remember I played the Scottish Fantasy. Afterwards he would talk about it with you, discussing how you'd played – but never in front of anyone.

KH No! He was far too kind to take anybody apart in front of their peers.

EH Quite unlike at least one other great teacher, who enjoyed taking people apart!

LB He had a delightful sense of humour.

NL I remember, when he was teaching at Bunty Lempfert's studio and used to go back and forth on the bus. The conductor said, "Is that an electric violin?" and Sascha said, "No! North Sea Gas!"

TR I remember when he was playing Last Rose of Summer to me and he looked up shyly, saying, "You know, if they had an International Competition for the over-eighties, I think I might win a prize!"

And one morning he was practising slowly in his drawing room – up in that second-floor flat – his famous exercise. Fourths between thirds as you gradually crawled up the strings. Suddenly a ladder appeared at the window, and there was the window cleaner. "All right if I do the windows?" And he got on with his work, with Sascha still practising slowly. When the cleaner had finished, he said, "How long have you been playing the violin?" Sascha replied, "All my life." The window cleaner retorted, "You've not got very far, have you?" Sascha commented afterwards, "You should have seen the look of pity on his face!"

TW We all remember his dear old war horses – Otello Fantasy, Last Rose of Summer and so on. I went to see him, about a month before he died, and he played all those things, wonderfully, still. And of course in the thirties he broadcast the Beethoven Sonatas – and Sammons wrote him a letter of congratulation.

LB I remember visiting him on his 80th birthday; I'd come from a rehearsal and had my violin with me. It was a Strad, and he asked to see it. Then I was asked to play – then "Give it to me," and he played the Sinding Suite and some Bach. Marvellous.

TR He was still smoking – and he told me not to!

ML He didn't inhale. But the cigarette was there – he had to have it out of the corner of his mouth. Like a sort of talisman.

NL We made a collection among his pupils for a present, and he was absolutely thrilled when we went to give him the cheque. Anything to do with his pupils always went straight to his heart.

KH I only had two lessons from him because family illnesses meant I had to stop playing for a while – but I do remember that I couldn't do string crossings and he made me play scales in broken thirds without any open strings. He wouldn't let me play open strings, and I found that very difficult.
   I remember his story about his old friend Elman, when he went backstage to see him on Elman's first post-war visit and said, "Well, Mischa! You still play well!" Elman replied, "What do you mean, still? What's on your mind?"

TW Sascha also used to tell about Elman, who left the Conservatoire when he was twelve to start his international career. He came back to the Conservatoire a few years later and Auer asked him to hear Heifetz. Asked for his opinion afterwards, all Elman could say was "Good technique." And that was that.

NL I always remember those photographs, the first things you saw when you went into his room – Auer amid his class, and

Elman's photo inscribed 'To Sascha from Mischa'.

TW That class, in St. Petersburg – with Poliakin, Zimbalist, Elman, Sascha, Maskoff, Maud Powell, Kathleen Parlow! I met her in Canada, and she told me that Auer used to say, "If I come to your place at 2.30 in the morning and wake you up, you must be able to play anything you've learned." Auer was very strict. He would throw people out if they hadn't prepared.

I began to realise that there was more to violin playing than reading books and theorising and so on, and so I asked Sascha for lessons, and this changed my attitude. I could rely on the little I could do, you know, and when I had to play I could do it. It didn't always work, but that was not Sascha's fault.

His approach was so amazingly quick and simple – and it just showed you what to do to make it happen. Musically. Tastefully.

TR I went abroad to study with a Hungarian teacher with whom I didn't really get on. He changed everything, and I believed you get the best out of a teacher if you do what they say. So I changed everything, and it really taught me discipline, because I can remember playing some Bach and I could play it his way, and I could play it my way the next second, which was completely different, bowing, fingering, everything. It was wonderful discipline. But I came back to London, and I tried to get my technique back, bow arm fine, left hand not so good. So I was a bit worried, because I was playing the concerts, proms and things and another pupil, Michael Jones, told me to go to Lasserson, so I did, and I played my party piece, and he said, "Play B flat major scale," which I did. And he said, "Why have you come?" and I told him I couldn't hold the violin comfortably. He said, "Oh, that's easy. Four easy moves." So he gave me the four easy moves and we tried it a couple of times. He said then, "Do you play the Tchaikovsky? Bring it to me in a fortnight's time." So I thought, I can't hold the fiddle, how am I going to play the Tchaikovsky? But within a week I was practising in front of the mirror, and I looked at myself, and I thought, I've seen that somewhere before.

And it was a picture of myself at the age of 5 playing the violin, and I looked like that. It brought me back to basics. Back to a system which was so practical, so simple.

NL All I can remember about my first lessons, quite honestly, was feeling happy that this was what I'd been looking for – as well as those photographs which I can see now, in that room in St Quintin's Avenue.

TR I can remember a feeling of such intense gratitude because Sascha had saved me from dropping the fiddle all over the place. I still do the system – and I teach it. One – there's a little button at the end of the violin. You see that there, and you put it centrally against your throat there, just like that. Central, just let it hang. Then you take the violin – I had a pupil who had a Strad, and he said, "I can't do this, I might destroy the violin." Take the violin, and angle it so that it hits your collar bone. There's no space there. Thirdly, you swing your arm like an underarm throw, the space is smaller, now you know how much shoulder rest you need, and where it should be, just be on the collar bone. And he said that the last thing you do is just drop your head; just drop it. And that's it. I kept doing that and it was so easy. It landed up in the right position.

TW Well, the basic things were very much with this principle of string crossing. According to Sascha's teaching, and I personally think it's absolutely right, when you are crossing strings and using separate bows, the whole arm goes up and down in one piece, the weight is dropped, and you cross all in one piece. If you are playing legato, then you use the wrist a little to help as well. He would also say little things like; when playing arpeggio over strings, as you cross the string at that split second you change string, use more bow, not less. There were all kinds of things, broken thirds he taught us all, four-octave scales, and the arpeggios. And also, not to come right the way round. People even with quite long thumbs like to leave the neck of the violin altogether and come up here, and then of course it's a problem how to get back. Whereas, he would say, what you did with the thumb in the low positions didn't matter, whatever was natural; but if you were going to play, say, A major four octaves arpeggio, thumb back to begin, and then the thumb would describe a diagonal line under the neck, and you would stay not far away from the edge of the fingerboard when you come up here, and to reach, you would flatten these fingers, and the stretch became easy and reliable, and you were able to get back down. It was there, you felt you could rely on it.

One thing he taught us all, I'm sure. You know this business that most people have of curling their fourth finger when they lift it. He was very strict about having the fingers over the string before you played, and you raised the finger above the note you just played before it went anywhere else. You change the whole arm level with the whole arm, and by practising broken 3rd scales you would put down two fingers each time: Da - de - da - ba etc, and you keep the shape of the hand aligned, and I can think of at least one great violinist who didn't always do that, and whenever he didn't, he played slightly out of tune. So I think Sascha was right in many ways.

NL Sascha wasn't rigid – he dealt with everybody according to their own problems.

TR But the basic thing, I think, I had a repeat programme with Lasserson. I always remember Menges saying, "You're weak. You've got no grip in your hand," which I had been pitied for, and I always thought it was a great advantage, because she said, "You've got to learn to do things the right way." I had to learn about throwing out the arm, I had to learn about what I did with the hand, and the leverage of the bow, and always she kept talking about point of contact, and Lasserson was always talking about the point of contact. And that really matters, how you stroke the strings. Whatever you do otherwise hardly matters, as long as you stroke the strings.

LB I met Sascha in Hill's one day. He was looking at some bows, and he persuaded me to try a Sartory. For a couple of days I didn't know what to make of it, then after a few more days I realised it was giving me something a bow had never done before. So, I bought it for £35.

EH I didn't have lessons from Sascha. I remember that in 1937 I went up to the Scottish Orchestra in Glasgow. The new young conductor was Georg Szell. The new leader was Henri Temianka, and I found that quite a lot of people there were having lessons from Temianka. I was 18 then, and he was a wonderful violinist, and I didn't have lessons from him because I felt it would be disloyal to my teacher, Sidney Rogers. A few months later, 1938, there was I playing with Sascha and I could see by the way he asked me to play things and looked at me that he would probably have liked to give me some lessons, and I would like to have had some. But once again I felt it would be disloyal to do that.

NL I remember the Bor family saying that, as a child, he played marvellously but he hadn't the extrovert manner of a prodigy. He was very shy, and would turn his back on the audience and wouldn't face them while he played.

LB I tried to persuade him to live and to teach in my house – in the top flat. But it was semi-detached and he was desperately worried about problems with neighbours complaining about the noise.

NL I remember a story Sascha told me about Auer being something of a tyrant. He used to sweep into the class and sit on a rostrum; the pupils would play, and the class would usually finish at four in the afternoon. Heifetz played through a recital programme one day, to tumultuous applause. Auer asked for someone else to play, but nobody dared – until one poor soul at the back volunteered, and Auer looked at the clock and said, "We'll finish early today!"

TR There was another story about some great national holiday in Russia: 'Freedom of the Serfs'. There were only two people in the Conservatoire that day. Auer had arranged a class, and Sascha was the only pupil to turn up. Afterwards, Auer would always give him a nudge and murmur, 'Freedom of the Serfs!'

He was such a kind gentle man, for whom everybody had the greatest respect. He certainly never taught through fear. He just encouraged the best in people.

NL Well, he was such a retiring person, and so generous. If I can just finish with the story – I mean, the fees he charged were ridiculous, I mean, totally ridiculous. When I first went to him he was charging 1 guinea for a lesson. And I had these lessons and then went back to him several years later and, when it came to the end of the lesson, I got my cheque book out and I said, "What is it now, Mr. Lasserson?" and he said, "Oh, it is 2 guineas, but, for you, thirty bob." And I thought, that absolutely summed him up. This generosity.

DL I want to thank everyone for coming – because I knew Sascha only when I was a tiny boy. Ever since then, total strangers have come up to me and said, "I knew him so well; it's a great pleasure to meet you," and I've never really known what it's all about, so for me it's a great learning process. My interest particularly, having studied a lot in the last few years, is in his specific system of teaching, and certainly today has been more enlightening than anything I have ever heard.

The Lassersons in Russia
by Ilya Fridman

In 1962, in what was then the Soviet Union, there was published Raaben's biography of Leopold Auer. The book included a list of the maestro's pupils, and among its names was that of Solomon Lasserson, who graduated from the St Petersburg Conservatoire in 1909 with the Silver Medal. It was not until 1994 that I discovered Solomon Lasserson was in fact Sascha Lasserson, the great violinist who left Russia in 1914 on a concert tour of England and whose return was prevented by the Great War and the Russian Revolution. Since then, his name has been almost unknown in Russia for a reason as simple as it is sad – to have relatives abroad could be dangerous for Soviet citizens.

Sascha left his mother, three sisters and a brother, and in 1918 – at the height of the Revolution and the Civil War – that family moved from their home in St Petersburg to Nizhni-Novgorod, a city in whose cultural development they were to play a major role. The city, renamed Gorki under the Soviets, is the third biggest in Russia. Balakirev was born there; Nicolas Rubinstein founded a Music College there, one of the oldest in the country; its Opera House was opened in 1930; the Music Academy opened in 1946; the Festival of Contemporary Music began in 1962, and the First International Scriabin Piano Competition was held in 1995.

The Lasserson family lived in a single room, divided into several sections on the city's main street. They supported each other in every way, and were devoted to their mother. They remained in the city for the rest of their lives, and are buried there. Of the four children, all were musicians except Raisa; she was trained as a Chemical Engineer and worked in one of the city's factories.

Ida was a pianist, devoting her life to teaching children. Anna, also a pianist, began her career as a child prodigy in St Petersburg; she studied with Dubasov, himself a pupil of Anton Rubinstein and a winner of the International Piano Competition founded by his teacher. Dubasov thought most highly of Anna's playing. She established a career in Nizhni-Novgorod as a concert soloist as well as a chamber music player and teacher. In the 1940s she gave up her concert career to concentrate on teaching, but she was remembered for her astonishing virtuosity and wonderful feeling for sound and rhythm. As a teacher she was as demanding of her pupils as she was of herself, yet remained remarkably sensitive and endlessly kind. She was loved and trusted by all her pupils who are now working all over Russia, and sharing with their pupils the ideals of their great teacher.

Semeon, Sascha's brother, represents in himself a whole era for the city. Like his brother, he was originally a fine violinist. He also graduated from the St Petersburg Conservatoire where he had studied with Nalbandian, one of Auer's favourite pupils. He started his concert career on arrival in Nizhni-Novgorod in 1918, and then became obsessed with the idea of conducting. In the aftermath of the chaos of Revolution and Civil War, he established the Radio Orchestra in the twenties, and some years later he established the Symphony Orchestra. This organisation was completely destroyed in the war, and Semeon rebuilt it in the 1940s together with a repertoire including much contemporary music.

Semeon and his Orchestra regularly attracted the finest of the country's musicians as soloists. As a conductor, he was immensely thorough at rehearsals; his work was imbued with passion and spirit, yet there was nothing flashy about his style. Semeon founded the city's Violin School. He worked in the Music College and the Academy. He taught the young musicians of the Student Orchestra with great care and patience and – as with his sister, Anna – his pupils are working all over the country.

Musically, he was the most important figure in the city for

decades, but – sadly – was not treated by the Soviet regime with the respect he deserved. He was given no artistic title, no professorship, and almost until the end of his life he had to live in a communal flat.

None of the Lassersons married, and so, in effect, their children were really that great army of young musicians who were taught and nurtured by them with such affectionate care. My own connection with the Lassersons goes back to my childhood. Ida Lasserson was my first piano teacher. Anna was almost a second mother to me. I continued my studies with her, and it was she who inducted me into the life of a professional musician. It was Semeon Lasserson who conducted my first ever performance of Rachmaninov's Third Concerto in 1961.

They were exceptionally hard-working, devoted to music, to their pupils, and to each other. They showed a fierce artistic independence, and were marvellously kind to their pupils. They were all great musicians, with total artistic integrity. As far as the city is concerned, their contribution to its musical life was immeasurable. As far as I am concerned, it remains one of the greatest privileges of my life to have known them.

Ilya Fridman is a pianist who studied in Nizhni Novgorod and Moscow. Presently Professor-consultant at Nizhni Novgorod Academy, he lives in Germany. Many of his pupils have won international competitions. He gives concerts throughout Russia and Europe.

Sascha's Memorial Concert

This was, above all, a pupils' concert in which some of the most distinguished members of the profession – all of whom had studied with Sascha – came together to play both as soloists and as a chamber ensemble in that same hall where he had given so many recitals over sixty years ago. The hall was, of course, packed with family and pupils and friends, and friends of pupils, as well as those who, while none of these, had come to share in this homage. The atmosphere was one of warmth and an affectionate sharing of memories of a man who had meant so much to so many musicians for so long. The printed programme was far more than just that for it contained, among other things, photographs of Sascha and other great musicians which appear elsewhere in this book.

We reproduce here the introduction – a review of Sascha's life and achievements – as well as the actual concert programme together with tributes from admirers, pupils, and friends, and a concert review.

SASCHA LASSERSON, HIS LIFE AND ACHIEVEMENTS
Trevor Williams

Sascha Lasserson was born in Vitebsk, Latvia, on May 1st 1890. His father, a professional violinist, gave him his first lessons when, at the age of five, his interest in the instruments hanging on the walls at home became apparent. He said later that he spent hours gazing at them and that everything about them fascinated him. When he was ten, he entered the St Petersburg Conservatoire as a pupil of Galkin, a pupil of Wieniawski and Vieuxtemps, and in that year he made his debut in Helsingfors; he played the Spohr Ninth Concerto with Robert Kajanus conducting. Later, with the same conductor, he played the Vieuxtemps Fifth Concerto in St Petersburg.

Before he was twelve he entered the class of the great Leopold Auer, where his fellow students included Elman, Parlow, Achron, Zimbalist, Seidel, Cecilia Hansen, Burgin, Borisov, and Heifetz – an unparalled array of talent. In 1909, he was awarded the Gold Medal Diploma and, two years later, he won the coveted Highest Distinction Award – open only to postgraduate students – for which all the solo sonatas of Bach had to be prepared. During this period he played Glazounov's Concerto in St Petersburg with the composer conducting. Here , and in other cities in Russia – and elsewhere – Kiev, Vilna, Riga, Warsaw – his concerts were received with great acclaim. After a performance of the Tchaikovsky Concerto a leading St Petersburg paper wrote; "He possesses the requisite artistic power and consummate technique, coupled with absolute lack of all apparent effort. He astounded by his masterful brilliance and profound depth of feeling. But technique is not his goal, only a means, and there is no doubt that Mr Lasserson will take his place among the virtuosi of the world."

In 1914, shortly before the outbreak of war, he arrived in this country, where his concerts were received with great enthusiasm. Newspaper reviews, letters of recommendation from Elman and Zimbalist, and congratulations from Albert Sammons for his performances of the Beethoven Sonatas for the BBC in the Twenties – all these attest to his achievements as an artist.

However, it was his other career as a teacher which was his most important contribution to music. He was a man of enormous kindness and patience; a person of rare humility, he sought to further the talents of others, rather than just his own. He was modest and gentle, and never spoke unkindly of his colleagues; his fees were never as much as they should have been, and he avoided any kind of self-indulgence or notoriety. Thus , his fame was confined to the musical world, where he became a household name –

especially, of course, among violinists. All the players, whose ambition it was to play the violin well, came to him, and it is a fact that most of the well-known violinists in this country have studied with Sascha Lasserson at some time.

To describe his method of teaching is difficult, as he would never approach any two pupils in the same way. Once, asked by a pupil for his philosophy of teaching, he said; " I try to imagine myself as each pupil, and to look at the problems from his or her point of view". His example was inspiring. He always practised every day; Bach, Paganini, Ernst, Ysaye, Vieuxtemps – and scales, and was practising and teaching until two days before his death

At lessons he was always ready to demonstrate any technical or musical point, even when advancing years had brought the pain and discomfort of rheumatism in hands and shoulders. He could still play wonderfully at eighty-eight, and to hear his Paganini (especially the Caprices 1, 4, and 24, the Moto Perpetuo, and the Sauret Cadenza from the D-major Concerto), Ernst's The Last Rose of Summer, Othello Fantasy, Hungarian Fantasy and the F-minor Concerto, Ysaye's Ballade, Bach's Fugues and Chaconne, the Cadenza of Glazounov's Concerto – or, indeed, any passage from almost any work in the repertoire, always from memory – was a remarkable experience. He retained his renowned control and facility until the end.

Heifetz, Elman, Milstein, and Zimbalist were his friends and, although his own career had not their kind of achievement, every-where he went he was much loved and greatly respected. He was always so happy when one of his pupils had played well and received a good notice, or when he had proved to them – at what-ever stage of their development – that they could do something they had never thought possible. That was the kind of success he valued most.

This afternoon's concert is being given by some of his pupils on behalf of all the violinists in this country and abroad, who have ever studied with this great man.

"I am happy to join in the tributes to a remarkable man, Sascha Lasserson. As a student, I enjoyed excellent guidance but there were a few items of technique which perplexed me. So it came about that I approached Mr Lasserson hoping that his legendary wisdom might be of service to a mere cellist.

So it proved to be, especially in the domain of bowing. I found his ideas on the staccato and string-crossing especially creative, all delivered with kindness and firmness, an ideal combination of qualities for teacher.

Stories of his selflessness towards students accord well with the man I encountered and I gratefully join the large circle of his admirers." *Christopher Bunting*

"I am proud to be associated with all the distinguished musicians who will join in this afternoon's tribute to the great teacher Sascha Lasserson. His long residence with us has been a most valuable addition to the musical resources of this country and he will be greatly missed." *Adrian C. Boult*

"I am happy to associate myself with this memorial concert. Sascha Lasserson was a much respected and admired colleague of mine over many years since we first met in the 1930's. I feel sure that his achievements will last for many years." *Alfredo Campoli*

"Sascha was a frequent visitor to our London premises for over fifty years, and will always be remembered with warmth and affection by all the members of our firm who came into contact with him." *Desmond Hill*

"Sascha was a great teacher, whose whole life was dedicated to the teaching of beautiful violin playing. To hear him play and demonstrate at lessons made one realise just how much more there was to learn. His criticism was always constructive. While understanding immediately a pupil's faults, and knowing exactly how to put them right, he was able to inspire the confidence in one's own ability to improve one's playing." *Margot MacGibbon*

"There is nothing more moving than the heartfelt tributes of students to their teachers. Although I cannot count myself among those many illustrious colleagues who have studied with Sascha Lasserson, I willingly join in tribute to a very great pedagogue, violinist, and humanitarian – for all great teachers must be, by definition, humanitarians." *Yehudi Menuhin*

"Mr Lasserson was a wonderful violinist and musician. He was also a wonderful person whom I loved and admired." *Nathan Milstein*

"During the transition period between being a student and becoming a full professional I was greatly indebted to Sascha Lasserson for the time he spent with me. Before recitals and occasional concerto performances, I found him to be an artist of impeccable classical taste. If I managed to win his approval I felt much safer in public! Knowing the stature of many of his contemporaries under Leopold Auer, I hardly expected him to be stunned by my technical prowess but he was continually supportive and encouraging, and helped me to gain in confidence. A quiet and gracious friend, he was a man of great artistic and technical integrity." *Colin Sauer*

"I remember Sascha Lasserson as a wonderful man whose work I greatly admired." *Marie Wilson*

(The tributes from Colin Sauer and Marie Wilson appeared in the Lasserson Centenary issue of 'The Strad', in December 1990, and are reproduced here by courtesy of 'The Strad')

MEMORIAL CONCERT PROGRAMME

MOZART *Divertimento in D, K138*
Allegro – Andante – Presto
Leader *Lionel Bentley:* Conductor *Antony Hopkins*

BACH *Violin Concerto in A-minor*
Allegro Moderato – Andante – Allegro Assai
Director and soloist *Carl Pini*

SCHUBERT *Adagio and Rondo in A for Violin and String Quartet*
Lionel Bentley, Anthony Howard, Marjorie Lempfert,
Peter Willison: Soloist *Nona Liddell*

BACH *Chaconne from Partita no.2 in D-Minor*
Soloist *Elisabeth Matesky*

ACHRON *Hebrew Melody for violin and piano*
Tessa Robbins and Antony Hopkins

MENDELSSOHN *Scherzo from the Octet*
Violins; *Lionel Bentley, Nona Liddell Tessa Robbins, Anthony Howard*
Violas; *Kenneth Essex, George Turnlund*
Cellos; *Christopher Bunting, Peter Willison*

INTERVAL

BACH *Brandenburg Concerto No.3 in G*
Allegro – Adagio – Allegro
Violins; *Nona Liddell, Meyer Stolow, Tessa Robbins*
Violas; *Kenneth Essex, Marjorie Lempfert, George Turnlund*
Cellos; *Peter Willison, Christopher Bunting, Anita Lasker*

BARTOK *Sonata for unaccompanied violin*
Tempo di Ciaccona – Fuga – Risoluto, non troppo vivo – Melo-
dia Adagio – Presto
Trevor Williams

TCHAIKOVSKY *Meditation*
RIMSKY KORSAKOV – ZIMBALIST *Fantasy Coq d'Or*
Alla Sharova and Antony Hopkins

SAMMARTINI – ELMAN *Canto Amoroso*
Max Jaffa and Antony Hopkins

TCHAIKOVSKY *Elegie and Valse from the Serenade for Strings, op 48*
Conductor *Antony Hopkins*

THE CONCERT *A hitherto unpublished review by Robert Lewin*

A large crowd gathered at the Wigmore Hall on January 7th, with
Lasserson pupils not only on the platform but among an audience
that had patiently queued up to be present at an historic occasion,
the launching of the Sascha Lasserson Scholarship Fund to com-
memorate a great man and continue his life's work. Unkind
weather conditions caused absentees among international entries

on the planned programme, while the problem of getting busy top-ranking players together for rehearsals obliged an omission or two among the concerted items – but the ensemble playing was of a remarkably high order, something that not only reflects the star status of the performers but also the musicianship that Lasserson inculcated in his pupils. It may be revealed that, besides the violinists, at least one of the cellists at this concert – Christopher Bunting – went to Lasserson.

Still, it was the violinists' day. Has there ever been a concert with so many brilliant solo players following one another with the orderly precision of a pupils' event? A celebrities' concert would be a more accurate description , and the proceedings began with the entire cast serenading the audience with Mozart's Divertimento in D, music brim-full of youthful Mozartian zest as if to signal that although this was styled a Memorial Concert it was to be no sad occasion. Lasserson, who – all through his life sought to arouse only hope and optimism among his disciples – would not have wished it otherwise. There are teachers who firmly implant the mark of their own precise violin method in their students so that you recognise, almost at a glance, "Ah, a pupil of So-and so, I see". Fitting each and every student into the same mould can be effective, given the person with just the right shaped physique; it makes life easier for the teacher, but no single fixed system is likely to serve all. Lasserson's way was the harder one of studying each pupil, analysing his special talents and his weaknesses, and providing the individual treatment and specialised tactics best for that person. Thus, nothing can be more different than your Lasserson pupils, an intriguing matter to observe among the succession of solo performers.

It is well known that Lasserson welcomed new pupils at any stage, from beginners to advanced professionals, and even concert artists of note would go to him to cure the violin ills to which we are all prone. Maybe the lucky ones were those who actually began with Lasserson, and I believe Carl Pini dates his association with Lasserson back to his very early violin days. He played and directed the Bach Concerto in A Minor, a vivid and exciting performance, the very antithesis of the placid – not to say jaded – kind of performance a classic work often tends to produce. Bach's string writing is nothing without the sense of momentum, and Carl Pini's attack and rhythmic control emphasised his gifts of leadership that never dominated in any obtrusive way but yet ignited the spirit of his entire group. Of course, you don't achieve that without matching support, and the ensemble pieces mostly had Lionel Bentley as leader to confer his kind of quiet distinction.

Nona Liddell played the Schubert Adagio and Rondo in A for solo violin and string quartet. This is a work most of us know only in the reduction for violin and piano; obviously, opportunities for a recitalist to have a string quartet handy must be rare, and there is little or no other repertoire for this combination. It was rewarding to hear the piece in the original setting and with a soloist renowned for the suave and stimulating beauty of her playing. This is an entertainment in Schubert's most joyous manner, and Nona Liddell's accomplished art included not only happy turns of phrasing but also something essential to Schubert, a full dynamic range.

Next came Tessa Robbins. How rarely, these days, do we hear this fine artist. She played that little masterpiece, Hebrew Melody by Achron, one of the set of eight pieces recorded by the fabulous Joseph Hassid. Comparisons are said to be odious but, since nobody has ever played like Hassid, perhaps no greater compliment can be paid to Tessa Robbins than to suggest that the seductive sheen of her sound was almost as haunting as that of Hassid himself.

The second half opened with Brandenburg no.3 in G and you don't often get a chance to hear nine players of this calibre convert the old warrior into a marvellously woven chamber music-sounding piece, probably just what Bach had in mind. Following that overture, no greater contrast could be imagined than a musical transformation scene into modern times with Trevor Williams playing the Bartok unaccompanied solo sonata. Even after 35 years, this work does not make easy listening, but it is superlative violin music laid out with the skill of a master's hand. Also, it takes virtuosic handling, with its contrasting moods exploiting the technical and tonal resources of the violin. This is a testing recital work, and a challenge of no mean order to come out and play it "from cold". Trevor Williams' vigorous approach had the firmness and conviction essential to the Bartok fugal manner, a mood quickly converted to the subtle mysteries of the lovely Melodia. But Trevor Williams is a decidedly versatile Lasserson scholar for, besides this impressive solo contribution, one must commend his interesting biographical note of Sascha Lasserson in the concert programme, which reveals data new to many of us.

After Bartok, we had Alla Sharova – who looks English but who comes from Russia. She studied with Dubinsky, of the Borodin Quartet, and with Lasserson when she arrived in London. She played two perennial favourites, the Tchaikovsky "Meditation" and Zimbalist's Fantasia on themes from Rimsky Korsakov's "Coq d'Or". An operatic selection these days has a nice touch of the days of yore about it, but this is a fine piece of violin idiom by one of the original Auer class (Zimbalist, who was born in 1889, was senior to Sascha). Alla Sharova has an admirable presence, and her tone has a radiant quality, smooth and memorable.

But, just when you might imagine you has exhausted every possible facet of Lassersonic variations, along came Max Jaffa. Like Albert Sandler before him, the sound of his violin is loved by millions of fans who might not have heard of Bartok, and he played the much loved Sammartini-Elman Canto Amoroso with a beguiling sweetness that bewitched his audience.

Finally, the graceful Tchaikovsky Waltz for Strings brought the music to a close. One must pay tribute to Antony Hopkins, who conducted; played the harpsichord well as the piano accompaniments; and spoke about Sascha Lasserson and the objects of the Fund. The concert was organised by Brian Underwood, who managed to persuade some of the busiest musicians in London and elsewhere to give their services, which amounted to rather more than just that because it meant giving up engagements. The concert raised over £600 for the Fund, and more has been contributed and promised. May the campaign to advance the Lasserson Scholarship Fund prosper!

My Uncle Sascha
Michael Lasserson

Perhaps paradoxically, my understanding and admiration of my Uncle Sascha is greater now – twenty years after his death – than during his lifetime. Since I began to work on the book, the various contributions – together forming a multi-faceted composite portrait of him as Artist, as Teacher, as Man – have told me more than I ever knew of his greatness, humility, and kindness. But, as I look back on my relationship with him, warm and loving as it was, I am injcreasingly aware of distance between us, and that not borne merely of age.

My own upbringing, that of a conventional English schoolboy – sport-loving and inarticulate, was light-years removed from that amazing hot-house which nurtured Sascha and his great contemporaries and was just as remote from that almost monastically severe discipline of study and practice which he embraced so devotedly, possibly more so than any other of Auer's pupils. It was this which endeared him to Auer, who recognised Sascha's understanding of violin playing as akin to his own, and who appointed him as Assistant or Monitor to his class. It was, of course, this profound understanding that equipped him so superbly, not only as an Artist but also as one of the greatest teachers of his generation. Again and again, in these pages, we learn of his incredible ability to assess and solve his pupils' problems both musical and technical, and his liberation of so many of those pupils from months and sometimes years of musculo-skeletal malfunction. We learn also of the tact and sensibility with which he approached such problems, always with recognition of the individuality of his pupils.

There was never any attempt to force a pupil into the straitjacket of conformity; rather was there discussion, advice, suggestion – and, unusually, recognition of a pupil's own ideas. There was no 'Sascha Stamp' on his pupils; rather was there – and, indeed, still is – a joy in being part of a fellowship of those privileged to study with him. They benefited from his generosity with his knowledge, his time, his concern for them, and of course from his ridiculously low fees (which he would raise only fractionally, and then with the greatest reluctance).

My own earliest memory of Sascha is of his delighted laughter on hearing me, as a very small boy, sing a theme from the Beethoven Concerto. He was kind and jolly, and was one of several uncles – and, as a child, I took him for granted as I did the others. I had no idea of his greatness, and such awareness dawned only slowly as I grew up and became used to the frequent and reverential greeting, "Are you related..?"

This awareness was enhanced by conversations with my father, who had been a fine violinist before reading Medicine. He knew Sascha well and admired him; indeed, it was with his family that Sascha stayed when he came to London in 1914 on a concert tour only to be trapped by the war and the Revolution, making his return to Russia impossible. My father used to say that Sascha's playing was of such purity that, if you stood next to him in a room while he was playing, you would hear nothing extraneous whatsoever, but only his amazing string sound. They would argue violinists and interpretation, for such talk was the breath of life to both. My father's opinions were savage and final, while Sascha would search for some redeeming feature before delivering his own far more gentle judgement.

Sascha loved any news and gossip about the violin world, and would get very excited about anything that he had heard – or had discovered for himself. I can recall his visit to us for lunch, and how he had barely taken off his coat before he burst out with his news. He had been listening again to some of Heifetz's recordings, and so – with eyes blinking behind his thick glasses, and cigarette dangling unlit – he started. "Chaifetz! You know?

Chaifetz!" (He never pronounced the name as 'Heifetz'.) Yes, we said, wondering just what all this was about. "Chaifetz!" he went on. "You know – Chaifetz! Chaifetz skretches!" Unbelievable, we replied. How could that be, with such machine-tooled perfection? But, Sascha was adamant. Heifetz did scratch (or skretch). And, for Sascha, this was news.

The rest of that day was spent with Sascha and my father arguing about a Russian violinist who had played in London for the first time. My father loudly dismissed him, proclaiming that he would not even cross the road to hear him if he played in London again. Sascha argued as best he could on the poor man's behalf, before eventually admitting that he, too, was unimpressed and also would not cross the road to hear another concert.

My own work, together with marriage and a young family, eventually made my visits to Sascha less frequent, but the welcome was always warm and affectionate; one stood on the doorstep and awaited that spruce, small figure coming down the long flights of stairs to beam his greeting at us. He was always interested to hear our news, but inevitably the talk would turn to music. As a musician, I was never anything other than a bad amateur – and not even a string player but I feel that he did recognise me as a sincere music lover and so was always ready to discuss players and performances, listening to me with the greatest courtesy, and never talking down to me.

Such musical discussions always led to Sascha demonstrating his arguments by playing, punctuating talk with superbly played quotations from the entire violin repertoire. This would almost invariably develop into something much greater as Sascha gradually absorbed himself in the music, and so one would be privileged to attend a private recital – as when he once played, for me alone, the Bach *Chaconne* in that small top-floor sitting room in St Quintin Avenue. Occasionally, he would recall his time in the Conservatoire, as when he told me how he had smuggled himself into the Great Hall to hear Mahler rehearsing the *Choral Symphony*.

He once heard me, as a teenager, trying to play a Bach Flute Sonata, something which, by Sascha's standards, I had no business even to attempt. He smiled, and put his arm round me, saying to my mother, "He phrases so musically." I felt myself warmed and somehow lifted onto a higher plane of musical achievement by that comment.

Sascha was a prodigy, as were his great contemporaries like Heifetz, Elman, Milstein, Maskoff, Zimbalist, Seidel and so many others. He achieved greatness early, as did they. He was awarded the highest honours his Conservatoire could bestow – and yet there seems nothing tangible of him that remains. Repeated efforts to trace something of him on film or video have so far led to nothing. He never recorded commercially, and there exists only a fragment of a Dvorak Slavonic Dance on cassette which can do no more than hint at his calibre as an Artist.

His contemporaries are recalled by film, video and huge discographies. Sascha is recalled by something else – intangible but perhaps far greater – the devoted affection and loyalty of his pupils and the honour in which he was held by all who knew him, as shown herein by the memories of the violinists he taught and helped so unstintingly. He embodied the great Auer tradition and he taught by Auer's methods, flavoured uniquely with his own vast experience and wisdom. He taught with kindness, understanding, humour. All this is apparent from the book as, sadly, is something else. Sascha was neglected by Official Musical Circles. There seemed to be no place for such a man in any of the music colleges, and even the attempt by his pupils to gain for him an Award in the Honours List came to nothing.

Sascha never restricted himself to teaching virtuosi. He accepted all on their merits, asking only for sincerity and commitment. Many of his pupils became famous as soloists and orchestral leaders, concert artists in their own right. Others played in the rank and file of the symphony orchestras. There were amateurs also, and Sascha took pride and pleasure in the achievements not only of those who reached the heights, but also of those who – after months of hard work – might manage a movement of a simple baroque sonata. It was this generosity of spirit which endeared him to so many.

I last heard him play shortly before he died. My cousin rang to say that Sascha had been a bit 'off colour' and perhaps I could drop in. I had not seen him for some time, and he looked frail and tired. The welcome was as warm as ever; we made tea and talked, first of family and then of music. Out came the violin, with Sascha suddenly and incredibly rejuvenated as he continued talking violins and violinists. He began to play, putting me through a crash course ranging over the entire repertoire, quizzing me as to the identity of excerpts from Bach *Chaconne*, Kreisler *Prelude* and *Rigaudon*, Brahms and Beethoven Concertos, Glazunov Concerto, *Last Rose of Summer*, *Otello Fantasy* – all played with a staggering power and fluency, belying the fact that he was only days from death. I came again the next night with my brother and cousin. Again, there was tea and talk and laughter. And, again, there was music, with the same amazing rejuvenating effect. One forgot the frailty and fatigue, for here surely was an artist at the very height of his powers.

We came again, two days later. He looked ill, and had taken to his bed. He needed more care than was possible at home, and we managed to get him into the local hospital. Much later that same day he died, gentle and uncomplaining to the last. It was one of his pupils, Brian Underwood, who summed it up so movingly – Sascha's long love affair with the violin was over.

Appendices

I thank Mr Brian Underwood for letting me have copies of the letters to Sascha from Mischa Elman and Efrem Zimbalist, and Miss Elisabeth Matesky for copies of the letters to her from Sascha.

I must thank Mr George Newman for his kindness in sending me a copy of part of the first movement of Tchaikovsky's violin concerto, reproduced here. It shows Sascha's markings in his own hand, which are specially of interest because they were originally those of Auer, who discussed the score with the composer himself. Also I must thank Mr Felix Pooler for sending me the Saint Saens Introduction and Rondo Capriccioso , also with Sascha's own markings and fingerings - again almost certainly based on those advised by Auer.

I must thank Miss Averil Carmalt for sending me Sascha's Warm-up and Flexibility Exercises, and Mr Felix Pooler for sending me the exercises written for him by Sascha, including some indications on how to practise Dont Study No. 1

LETTERS FROM MISCHA ELMAN AND EFREM ZIMBALIST

Mr. Sascha Lasserson is in my opinion a highly accomplished Artist and excellent teacher and those that are interested in Auer method should certainly seek the advice of Mr. Lasserson.

Mischa Elman

Temple Bar 4343

SAVOY HOTEL,
LONDON.

Nov. 20ᵗʰ.

It gives me very great pleasure
to recommend my old friend Sacha
Lasserson who is a first rate
violinist and teacher of the old
Auer's school. None better can be
found.

Efrem Zimbalist

1938.

TWO LETTERS FROM SASCHA TO
ELISABETH MATESKY

excuse my writing.

60 St. Quintin Ave.
London W. 10
June 1-75

My dear Elizabeth,
          Many thanks for
your letters, the last one
seemed more cheerful.
I was very glad to hear
from you. I hope that you
and Allen have settled down
Forgive me for not writing
sooner, my eldest son is quite
ill in Hospital, I am naturally
worried about him. I am very
glad to hear you have got
some concerts to play in future
                              T.O

~~what~~ What violin do you ~~do you~~ use now? —

My advice to you is to practise, the violin, play quarttets, trios and mix with people.

You have a very great talent, & you are a fine musician I am sure as time goes on ~~I so~~ you will play better and better and you will have a very big success

give my best wishes to Allen

With love

Sascha Lasserson.

My best wishes to your ~~parents~~

Michael love sends his to Dan Beth

August 12-1975
60 St-Quintin Ave
W. 10

My best wishes to
your parents.
Michel sends
his kind regard

My dear Elizabeth,

Many thanks for your letters
I hope everything will turn out as
you hope It would be simply —
marvellous for you to play in so many
different Countries and meet so many
people. My son Leon is much better
Thank God, but he is still a sick
person. I am teaching as usual.

There are so many of my pupils
talking about you and waiting

to hear you play again in London

I am sure if you play at Wigmore
hall you will have a big appreciate
audience all my friends and pupils
are asking when you are coming
to play in London. I am sure you
will have a very big success
My advice is to be cheerful and
happy and get a big repertoire,
Concertos, Sonatas & small
pieces
I am very pleased that Alben
is busy and studying. He will be
very happy if you make a name for
Yourself   with best wishes & love
              Sascha Lasserson

EXCERPT FROM THE 1ST MOVEMENT OF
TCHAIKOVSKY'S VIOLIN CONCERTO
WITH SASCHA'S FINGERINGS

Allegro giusto

SAINT SAENS 'RONDO CAPRICCIOSO'
WITH SASCHA'S FINGERINGS

VIOLON.

D. & F. 2041

VIOLON.

D. & F. 2041

VIOLON.

D. & F. 2041

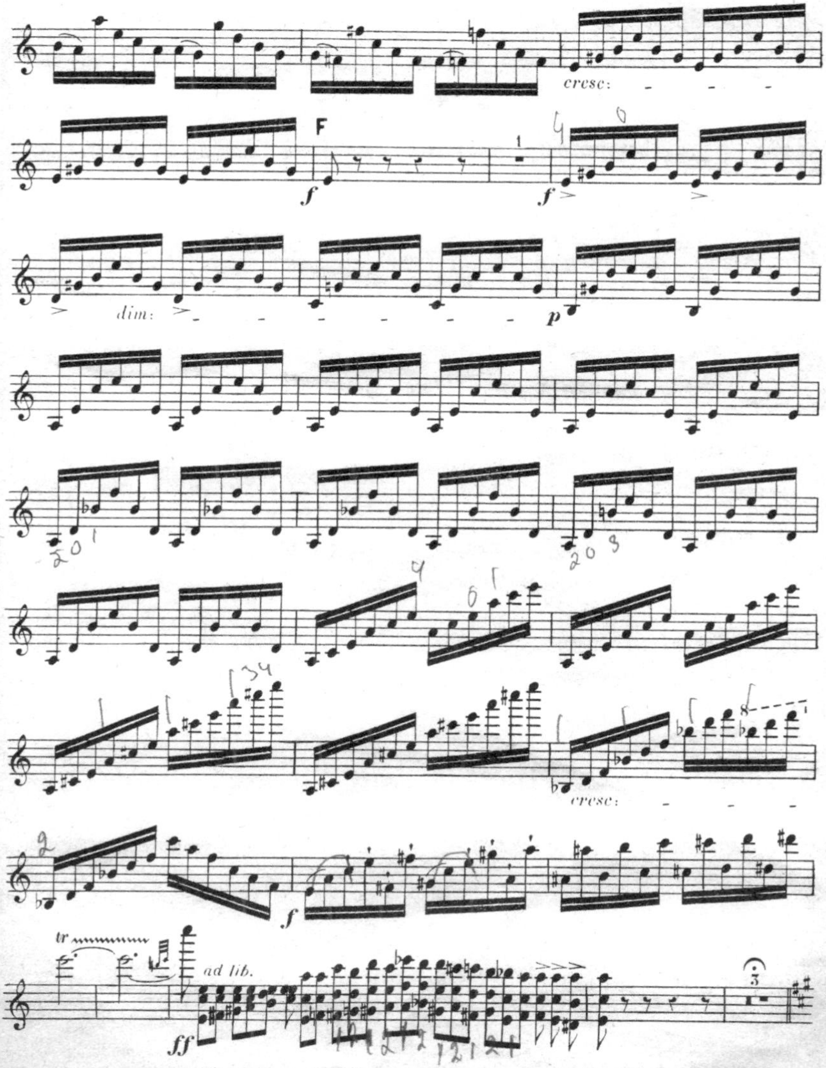

D. & F. 2041

VIOLON.

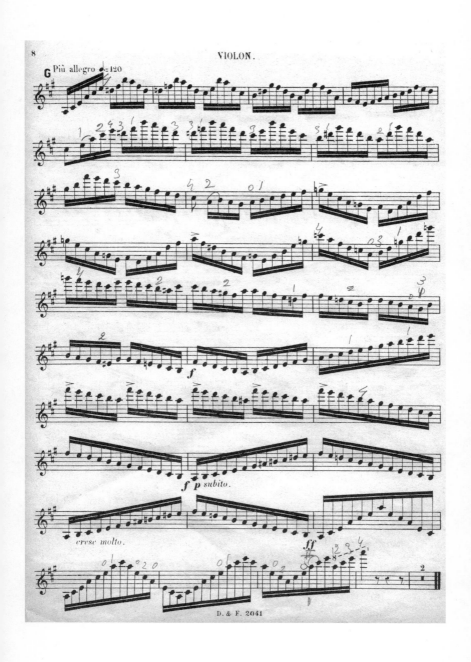

D. & F. 2041

EXCERPTS FROM DONT STUDY NO 1
WITH SASCHA'S FINGERINGS

SASCHA'S EXERCISES FOR 'WARM-UP & FLEXIBILITY' AND 'INDEPENDENCE OF FINGERS'

warm up and flexibility

Later all in one bow

Exercise for independence of fingers

SOME WIGMORE HALL RECITAL

PROGRAMMES

14th April 1917 Joint Recital with ADOLPH RAIBIN (Tenor) acc.
HAROLD CRAXTON

Concerto	*Paganini*
Chanson Louise XIII	*Couperin/Kreisler*
Theme & Variations	*Tartini/Kreisler*

9th June 1917 Charity Concert in Aid of League of Mercy with several artists; acc. PERCY KAHN

Ave Maria	*Schubert*
Theme & Variations	*Tartini/Kreisler*
Chanson Louise XIII	*Couperin/Kreisler*
Melodie	*Tchaikovsky*

9th April 1918 Joint Recital with ADOLPH RAIBIN (Tenor)

Deuxieme Rêverie	*Auer*
Spanish Dance	*Sarasate*
Nocturne	*Chopin*
Perpetuum Mobile	*Novacek*

November 1918 Three Recitals accompanied by LONIE BASCHE

Concerto	*Paganini*
Chaconne	*Bach*
Two Hebrew Melodies	*Achron*
Humoreske	*Aulin*
Zephyr	*Hubay*
Nocturne	*Chopin*
Spanish Dance	*Sarasate*

Concerto	Elgar
Sicilienne	Bach
Caprice Viennois	Kreisler
Moment Musical	Schubert
Hungarian Dance	Brahms
Theme & Variations	Corelli

Sonata	Lazzaroi
Concerto	Glazunov
Romance	Lewis
Perpetuum Mobile	Novacek
Melodie	Tchaikovsky
Ronde des Lutins	Bazzini

1st January 1919 Charity Concert in Aid of Jewish Workers Emergency Relief Fund. Several artists accompanied by LONIE BASCHE

Trio	Rosovsky
Hebrew Melody	Achron
Hebrew Song	Levenson

1st February 1919 Joint Recital with ANNA FILIPOVA (Soprano) acc. HAROLD SAMUEL

Variations	Tartini/Kreisler
Humoreske	Dvorak
Meditation – Thais	Massenet
Zephyr	Hubay

10th March 1919 Recital, accompanied by LONIE BASCHE

Kreutzer Sonata	Beethoven
Concerto	Mendelssohn
Melodie	Frank Bridge
Hungarian Dances	Brahms
Moment Musical	Schubert
Berceuse	Sammons
Ronde des Lutins	Bazzini

24th May 1919 Recital, accompanied by LONIE BASCHE

Sonata in E	Handel
Chaconne	Bach
Sonata	Elgar
Rondo Capriccioso	Saint-Saens
Chanson Louis XIII	Couperin/Kreisler
Sicilienne –	Francour/Kreisler
Scherzo	Kreisler
Hungarian Dance	Brahms

5th July 1919 Recital, accompanied by LONIE BASCHE

Sonata in C minor Op.30 No.2	Beethoven
Sonata	Elgar
Sonata	Lazzaroi

5th December 1919 Recital, accompanied by LONIE BASCHE

Sonata 'Devil's Trill'	Tartini
Symphonie Espagnole	Lalo
Romance in G	Beethoven
Sicilienne & Rigaudon	Francour/Kreisler
Gavotte	Aulin
Hungarian Fantasy	Auer

15th December 1921 Recital, accompanied by HAROLD CRAXTON

Sonata No.2	Ireland
Concerto 1st Movement	Tchaikovsky
Le Coq d'Or	Rimsky-Korsakov
Meditation	Glazunov
Valse from Ballet Raymonda	Glazunov
Caprice Viennois	Kreisler
La Chasse	Cartier/Kreisler
Schön Rosmarin	Kreisler
Hungarian Rhapsody	Auer

BROADCAST RECITALS

ACCOMPANIED BY LONIE BASCHE

11th January 1930 4.45 pm 5GB Daventry Experimental Programme

Romance in G	*Beethoven, arr. Wilhelmj*
Variations on theme	
by Corelli	*Tartini, arr. Kreisler*
Serenade	*Drigo, arr. Auer*
Valse Bluette	*Drigo, arr. Auer*
Second Rêverie	*Auer*
Zephir	*Hubay*
Slow Dance in E	*Dvorak, arr. Kreisler*
Perpetuum Mobile	*Novacek*

9th September 1930 9.20 pm London Regional Programme

Hebrew Melody	*Achron*
Zapateado	*Sarasate*
Polonaise in A	*Wieniawski*

(Solos in programme by the Wireless Military Band)

31st March 1931 7.50 pm National Programme

Meditation	*Glazunov*
Scherzo Tarantelle	*Wieniawski*

(Solos in programme by the Wireless Military Band)

4th August 1931 4.00 pm National Programme

Sonata for Violin & Piano	*Cesar Franck*

16th November 1931 3.45 pm National Programme

Sonata for Violin & Piano	*Richard Strauss*

26th April 1932 6.35 pm London Regional Programme

Praeludium and Allegro	*Pugnani, arr. Kreisler*
Tango	*Albeniz, arr. Kreisler*
Gavotte and Musette	*Tor Aulin*
Melodie	*Tchaikovsky*
Sicilienne and Rigaudon	*Sarasate*

(*Solos in programme by the Wireless Military Band*)

12th June 1932 12.30 pm National Programme

Sonata in E major	*Handel*
Sicilienne	*Bach / Auer*
La Capriceuse	*Elgar*
Polonaise in A	*Wieniawski*

15th September 1932 2.00 pm National Programme

Sonata for Violin & Piano	*Busoni*

6th March 1933 3.00 pm National Programme

Sonatina in D	*Schubert*
Sonata for Violin & Piano	*Debussy*

18th December 1933 4.00 pm National Programme

Sonata for Violin & Piano in G minor	*Brahms*

7th August 1934 4.40 pm London Regional and National Programme

Sonata for Violin & Piano in F major Op.24	*Beethoven*

7th September 1934 4.00 pm National Programme

Sonata for Violin & Piano "Kreutzer"	*Beethoven*

3rd December 1934 4.00 pm National Programme

Sonata for Violin & Piano in C minor Op.30, No.2	*Beethoven*

18th February 1935 4.00 pm National Programme

Sonata for Violin & Piano in G major Op.96	*Beethoven*

HILL'S CERTIFICATE OF SASCHA'S VIOLIN

TELEGRAMS — STRADIVARI, LONDON.
TELEPHONE — 0474 MAYFAIR.

William E. Hill & Sons,
Violin Makers, Repairers & Experts,
140, *New Bond Street,*
*London. W.*1   23rd June,   19 47.

ALBERT PHILLIPS HILL
PAUL EBSWORTH HILL
DESMOND BARTREY HILL

TRADE MARK.
The Sign of
JOSEPH HILL *in 1762.*

WE CERTIFY that the violin sold by us to S. Lasserson, Esq., of 60 St. Quintin Avenue, N. Kensington, W.10., was made by Spiritus Sorsana of Cuneo and bears a label dated 1737.

DESCRIPTION. The back in one piece of wood marked by a handsome small curl, that of the sides and head is similar. The table of pine of very fine grain at the centre opening slightly on the flanks and the varnish of a rich texture, of a light golden - brown colour.

This instrument is a characteristic example of the maker's work and in an excellent state of preservation. It is numbered R. 226 on our books.

William E. Hill & Sons

SASCHA'S MEMORIAL CONCERT

PROGRAMME

WIGMORE HALL
WIGMORE STREET, LONDON, W.1
Manager: WILLIAM LYNE

SASCHA LASSERSON
MEMORIAL CONCERT
SUNDAY, 7th JANUARY 1979 at 3 p.m.

Artists will include:
Lionel Bentley, Max Jaffa,
Anthony Howard, Nona Liddell,
Elisabeth Matesky, Carl Pini,
Tessa Robbins, Alla Sharova,
Meyer Stolow, Trevor Williams,
Kenneth Essex, Marjorie Lempfert,
George Turnlund, Christopher Bunting,
Olga Hegedus, Peter Willison,
Antony Hopkins.

Photo: DESMOND HILL

PROGRAMME

BACH	—	Concerto for violin in a-minor
		Brandenburg concerto No. 3 in G
		Chaconne from Partita No. 2 in d-minor
BARTOK	—	Sonata for violin - solo

*and works by **Mozart, Schubert, Mendelssohn, Achron,**
Rimsky-Korsakov-Zimbalist, Sammartini-Elman, Tchaikovsky.*

SASCHA'S DIPLOMA, THE HIGHEST DISTINCTION AWARD

Sascha's Diploma, granted by the St Petersburg Conservatoire of the Imperial Russian Musical Society, marks his transition from a Jew restricted in movement and domicile in Tsarist Russia, surviving as a pupil at the Conservatoire only as long as he was able to maintain his outstanding achievements – to a Jew who was a free citizen, able to travel throught the country as and when he wished, and recognised as a great artist. The diploma was signed by the Patron of the Society, Countess Elena Altenburgskaya and by Glazunov, the Director of the Conservatoire. The text reads:

DIPLOMA

The Arts Council of the St Petersburg Conservatoire of the IMPERIAL Russian Musical Society hereby certifies that **Shlom Leibovich Lazerson**, a Jew from Vitebsk, born 1 May 1890, has studied violin at the St Petersburg Conservatoire (under Professors *Galkin* and *Auer*) and has graduated in music, having completed all the requirements of the course and achieved the following results in the final examinations:

Main specialist subject:
    violin (under the esteemed Professor *Auer*)   Distinction

Secondary (compulsory) subjects:
    theory of music, instrumentation,
    history of music and aesthetics.   Merit

Piano   Pass

Viola   Highly Commended

General Studies: successful completion of a variety of courses taught at the Conservatoire.

In recognition of this, in accordance with statutes 71 and 73 of the Conservatoire of the IMPERIAL Russian Musical Society, and following the decision on 8 May 1909 by the Arts Council of the St Petersburg Conservatoire, the Chairman of the IMPERIAL Russian Musical Society has pleasure in conferring upon Shlom Lazerson the diploma of FREE ARTIST. In recognition of his special talent he is awarded a *silver medal*. To certify this, we present **Shlom Lazerson** on this 1st day of September 1909 with this diploma, signed and stamped by the St Petersburg Conservatoire.

CHAIRMAN OF THE SOCIETY   ....

DIRECTOR OF THE CONSERVATOIRE   *A. Glazunov*

MEMBERS OF THE COUNCIL   ....

Index

Many will read this book to refresh their own memories of Sascha, seen through the eyes of their colleagues. Others, who might not have studied with him, will wish to learn of him as man and artist, and to gain some insight into his teaching. This brief index indicates his ideas on teaching – not only the technical aspects (what he once referred to as the 'How' of violin playing), but also the philosophy behind his teaching. Sascha once summed all this up when he said: "All that I tell you is not mine. It is what I learned from Auer" (flavoured and modified, of course, by his own experience). This index serves, therefore, as a guide to his teaching, and takes us back – through Sascha – to the teaching of Auer himself.